Clean Code Mastery: Writing Maintainable and Scalable Software

A Step-by-Step Guide to Writing Clean, Readable Code

MIGUEL FARMER

RAFAEL SANDERS

All rights reserved

No part of this book may be reproduced, distributed, or transmitted in any form or by any means without the prior written permission of the publisher, except in the case of brief quotations embodied in critical reviews and certain other noncommercial uses permitted by right law.

Table of Content

TABLE OF CONTENTS

INTRODUCTION

Clean Code Mastery: Writing Maintainable and Scalable Software

In the fast-paced world of software development, writing clean, maintainable, and scalable code has never been more important. As systems grow in size and complexity, the ability to write **readable**, **efficient**, and **easily extendable** code becomes a fundamental skill for every developer. Yet, achieving this goal is not always straightforward. In a field where deadlines are tight, features are frequently added, and systems constantly evolve, maintaining a **high standard of code quality** can be challenging. That's where the principles of **clean code** come in.

This book, *Clean Code Mastery: Writing Maintainable and Scalable Software*, is designed to help you master the art of writing clean, readable, and efficient code that not only meets current requirements but is also prepared for future scalability and ease of maintenance. Whether you're a **beginner** looking to understand the foundations of clean code, or an **experienced developer** striving to refine your practices and adopt the latest techniques, this book is a comprehensive guide to writing code that stands the test of time.

Why Clean Code Matters

The quality of code is often the difference between the success and failure of a software project. **Clean code** isn't just about making code look neat—it's about making it **maintainable**, **scalable**, and **testable**. As software systems grow, messy, unstructured code can become a burden, leading to **increased bugs**, **hard-to-find errors**, **longer development cycles**, and **higher maintenance costs**. Clean code, on the other hand, enables faster **iterations**, **easier debugging**, and smoother collaboration among developers.

A key aspect of clean code is its ability to **adapt to change**. In today's software landscape, change is constant. New features, bug fixes, and architectural changes are introduced regularly. Clean code makes these changes possible with minimal friction. By maintaining clear **modularization**, **well-defined interfaces**, and **simple design**, you ensure that your codebase can evolve without becoming a **legacy burden**.

Moreover, clean code serves as the foundation for creating **scalable** applications. Scalability isn't just about ensuring that your application handles more users or processes more data—it's also about ensuring that the code itself can grow in size, complexity, and functionality without becoming unwieldy.

14

What You Will Learn in This Book

This book is divided into **27 comprehensive chapters**, each focused on a specific aspect of writing clean, maintainable, and scalable code. Whether you're working on **small projects** or **large enterprise systems**, you will learn valuable techniques and practices that are applicable across all scales of development.

- **Chapter 1: Introduction to Clean Code** lays the groundwork by defining clean code and explaining its importance. You will understand the long-term value of writing clean code and how it benefits both developers and the business.

- **Chapter 2: The Fundamentals of Clean Code** introduces core principles like simplicity, clarity, and the avoidance of duplication—principles that will help you write code that is easier to read, maintain, and debug.

- **Chapters 3–5** dive deep into **functions**, **variables**, and **classes**, showing you how to design and structure them to enhance code readability and minimize unnecessary complexity.

- **Chapter 6: The SOLID Principles** provides a comprehensive guide to some of the most important object-oriented design principles, teaching you how to write scalable and flexible code that can adapt as your project grows.

- **Chapters 7–10** cover more advanced topics like **avoiding code smells, refactoring**, and **unit testing**, with a focus on continuous improvement and the importance of maintaining code quality throughout the software development lifecycle.

- **Chapter 11–14** focus on how to **optimize** your code for both **performance** and **readability** without sacrificing one for the other.

- **Chapter 15–17** highlight the importance of **team collaboration** in clean code, showing you how to integrate clean code practices into your team's workflow, including the use of **code reviews, CI/CD pipelines**, and **documentation**.

- **Chapters 18–23** cover more specialized topics, such as **working with legacy systems, writing clean APIs**, and **using functional programming** techniques, providing you with a diverse set of tools for different development challenges.

- **Chapters 24–27** examine how modern trends in **AI, machine learning**, and **new software architectures** are influencing clean code practices, ensuring that your skills stay relevant in the future of development.

Why This Book is Different

While many books discuss clean code in the abstract, this one provides **real-world examples** and practical strategies for implementing clean code in your day-to-day work. You'll see how clean code practices can be applied to **large-scale systems**, **legacy codebases**, and **modern development environments**. Each chapter includes **hands-on examples, case studies**, and **step-by-step instructions** for applying the concepts in real-world scenarios.

This book goes beyond theory and helps you:

- **Understand and apply core principles** of clean code in practical scenarios.
- Learn **how to refactor legacy code**, incrementally improving code quality without disrupting ongoing work.
- Explore how modern tools like **IDEs, linters**, and **continuous integration pipelines** can help automate and enforce clean code practices in your workflow.
- Gain insights into how **collaboration** and **communication** within development teams contribute to writing clean code at scale.

Whether you're working on a **small startup project** or a **massive enterprise system**, this book provides the tools, principles, and methodologies needed to write **clean, efficient, and scalable code**.

17

Who This Book Is For

This book is for anyone interested in improving their ability to write clean, maintainable, and scalable code. Whether you're just starting out in software development or you're a seasoned developer looking to refine your practices, this book offers valuable insights and actionable steps.

- **Beginners** will gain a clear understanding of clean code principles and learn how to apply them from the very beginning of their coding journey.
- **Intermediate developers** will deepen their knowledge of clean code and learn advanced techniques for refactoring, testing, and maintaining large codebases.
- **Expert developers** will find new strategies for **optimizing code** and **scaling systems** while also discovering how emerging technologies, like **AI** and **machine learning**, are influencing the future of clean code.

Conclusion

Writing clean code is an essential skill for modern software developers. It allows you to build software that is **reliable**,

scalable, and **easy to maintain**—attributes that are crucial in today's fast-moving and competitive development landscape. In this book, we aim to provide you with the tools, principles, and strategies to elevate your coding practices and produce software that stands the test of time. By mastering clean code, you will not only improve your technical skills but also increase your ability to collaborate effectively with teams, deliver high-quality products, and contribute to the long-term success of the software projects you work on.

Let's begin this journey toward **clean code mastery**, where simplicity, readability, and maintainability meet the demands of modern software development.

CHAPTER 1

INTRODUCTION TO CLEAN CODE

Writing clean, maintainable code is a foundational skill for any software developer. Clean code is more than just working code—it is code that is well-organized, easy to understand, and easy to change or extend. This chapter will introduce the concept of clean code, why it is important for software maintainability and scalability, and the differences between clean code and "good enough" code. We'll also discuss how writing clean code can foster better collaboration within development teams and the potential consequences of neglecting code quality.

What is Clean Code?

Clean code refers to code that is written in a way that is **easy to read**, **easy to understand**, and **easy to modify**. It is code that expresses the developer's intent clearly, avoiding unnecessary complexity. In essence, clean code is code that makes a developer's job easier when they revisit it in the future or when another developer has to maintain it.

Key characteristics of clean code include:

- **Readability**: The code is easy to follow, with appropriate comments (where necessary) and well-chosen names for variables, functions, and classes.
- **Consistency**: The code follows standard conventions, and patterns are applied consistently throughout the project.
- **Simplicity**: Clean code avoids unnecessary complexity. The simpler the code, the easier it is to test, debug, and extend.
- **Modularity**: Code is broken down into smaller, manageable components that do one thing well. This makes the system easier to understand and maintain.

Why Clean Code Matters for Maintainability and Scalability

Writing clean code has a direct impact on the **maintainability** and **scalability** of a software project.

1. Maintainability

In the real world, code doesn't just run once and then disappear. It is **maintained**, **extended**, and **refined** throughout the software lifecycle. Clean code allows:

- **Easy updates**: When the code is clean, it's easier to implement new features or fix bugs without breaking existing functionality.

- **Faster debugging**: Clean code minimizes the number of **logical errors**, making it easier to find the root cause of a bug.
- **Code reviews**: Clean code makes it easier for other developers to **review** and **understand** your code, leading to fewer errors and faster iterations.

2. Scalability

Scalable code is code that can grow over time—whether through adding new features, handling more data, or processing more requests. Clean code enables scalability because:

- **Easier refactoring**: As projects grow, the need for refactoring increases. Clean code is designed with **refactoring** in mind, meaning changes and extensions can be made without disrupting the entire system.
- **Modularity**: A modular approach allows developers to add new functionality or change existing components without major changes to the entire system.
- **Performance optimization**: Writing clean code ensures that performance bottlenecks are easier to identify and optimize, particularly when dealing with large systems.

In both maintainability and scalability, the key takeaway is that clean code is **future-proof**—it remains understandable and flexible as projects grow, evolve, and require further development.

The Consequences of Writing Messy Code

While it might seem like a shortcut in the short term, writing messy code can cause serious problems in the long run. Messy code refers to code that is difficult to read, understand, and modify. The consequences of messy code include:

1. Increased Bugs and Errors

Messy code often results in hard-to-find bugs because it lacks clarity and structure. Developers may accidentally introduce errors when making changes, as they might not fully understand the code they're modifying.

2. Slower Development Cycles

As the codebase grows, the lack of structure in messy code means that new features or fixes are harder to implement. Developers may need more time to figure out how different parts of the system interact, resulting in longer development times.

3. Higher Technical Debt

Technical debt is the cost of taking shortcuts in the development process. Messy code is a form of technical debt, and just like financial debt, it accrues interest over time. Eventually, it requires more time and effort to **refactor** or **fix** than it would have to write clean code in the first place.

4. Difficulty in Onboarding New Developers

When new developers join a project with messy code, they may struggle to understand how the system works. This can lead to longer ramp-up times, slower progress, and increased likelihood of mistakes.

5. Reduced Collaboration

Messy code creates confusion in teams, leading to poor collaboration. When developers cannot understand each other's code easily, they're less likely to work together effectively, leading to silos and miscommunication.

Clean Code vs. "Good Enough" Code

In many development environments, there's a temptation to write **"good enough" code**—code that works but isn't optimized for readability or maintainability. The goal of writing **clean code** is to go beyond what's "good enough." Here's how they differ:

1. Focus on Long-Term Quality

- **Clean code** is written with the future in mind. It's designed to be easy to change and extend, even as the software evolves.
- **"Good enough" code** works for now but often leads to issues down the line. While it may fulfill requirements today, it can become harder to maintain and extend in the future.

2. Flexibility

- **Clean code** allows the software to evolve with minimal cost, whether it's refactoring, debugging, or adding features.
- **"Good enough" code** often locks the system into a particular structure or approach that can hinder change.

3. Readability and Understanding

- **Clean code** is intuitive, with clear variable names, well-organized functions, and concise logic.
- **"Good enough" code** may be functional but often lacks clarity, making it difficult for others (or even the original author) to understand later.

4. Code Longevity

- **Clean code** ensures the software remains valuable and maintainable over time, allowing it to last for years.
- **"Good enough" code** may be acceptable in the short term but will likely require extensive rework as the project grows.

How Clean Code Enhances Collaboration in Teams

Clean code is not just about writing software that works—it's about making the software accessible, understandable, and maintainable for everyone on the team. Here's how clean code enhances collaboration:

1. Easier Code Reviews

Clean code allows developers to conduct **effective code reviews**. When the code is well-structured and easy to read, it's easier for reviewers to understand and provide feedback. The result is fewer errors and faster iterations.

2. Clearer Communication

With clean code, developers communicate their intentions clearly. The names of functions, variables, and classes speak for themselves, making it easier for other developers to understand the purpose of each part of the system.

3. Faster Onboarding

New team members can get up to speed quickly when the code is clean. They won't have to waste time figuring out what the code does or how the system is structured. This leads to **shorter ramp-up times** and more productive team members.

4. Better Debugging and Maintenance

When bugs arise, clean code makes it easier to identify the problem. Developers can quickly find the relevant code, understand its purpose, and determine the cause of the issue. This leads to faster bug fixes and **more efficient problem-solving**.

5. Foster a Culture of Quality

When clean code is the standard in a development team, it sets a **quality benchmark** for everyone. It encourages developers to write code that is not only functional but also clean and maintainable, leading to better overall team productivity.

Conclusion

Writing clean code is an investment in the long-term success of a software project. Clean code ensures **maintainability**, **scalability**, and **team collaboration**, all of which are essential for building robust and reliable software. In contrast, writing "good enough" code may solve immediate problems but can result in long-term headaches and inefficiencies. By focusing on clean code practices, you not only improve the quality of your own work but also contribute to a healthier, more efficient development environment for your entire team. As we move forward in this book, you'll learn the techniques, principles, and practices that will enable you to consistently write clean, maintainable code that stands the test of time.

CHAPTER 2

THE FUNDAMENTALS OF CLEAN CODE

In this chapter, we'll lay the groundwork for writing **clean code** by covering the fundamental principles that every developer should embrace. Clean code is not just about making the program work—it's about making the codebase understandable, maintainable, and extensible over time. Writing clean code is a habit that can be cultivated with a deep understanding of core principles, simple techniques, and consistent practices. In this chapter, we will explore the **principles of clean code**, the importance of **readable variable names and functions**, how to use **code comments effectively**, and the role of **consistent formatting and style guides**.

Principles of Clean Code

1. Simplicity and Clarity

The first principle of clean code is to **keep it simple**. Simple code is easy to understand, modify, and extend. Simplicity doesn't mean writing fewer lines of code—it means removing complexity without losing the clarity or purpose of the code.

Why simplicity matters:

- Simplicity ensures that the code is easy to maintain and debug.
- Simple code avoids unnecessary logic and over-engineering.
- Simple code is more likely to be correct because it's easier to test, reason about, and review.

To achieve simplicity:

- **Avoid unnecessary abstractions**: Keep your abstractions simple. Don't introduce complex designs or frameworks when simple solutions exist.
- **Eliminate unnecessary complexity**: If a solution requires multiple steps or complex logic that doesn't provide clear value, reconsider the approach.

Example: Simple vs. Complex Code

Complex Code:

```cpp
int calculateArea(double length, double width) {
    double area;
```

30

```
    if (length <= 0 || width <= 0) {
        return -1;  // Invalid dimensions
    } else {
        area = length * width;
    }
    return area;
}
```

Simple Code:

```cpp
double   calculateArea(double   length,   double
width) {
    if (length <= 0 || width <= 0) return 0.0;
// Return 0 if invalid dimensions
        return length * width;
}
```

In the second example, the code is simpler because it directly returns the result without unnecessary logic.

2. Avoiding Duplication

One of the key principles of clean code is to **avoid duplication**. **Duplicate code** is harmful because:

- It leads to multiple places where changes must be made when fixing a bug or adding a feature.

31

- It introduces inconsistency in the codebase, making it harder to maintain and extend.
- It increases the chances of errors as the same logic may not be updated uniformly across different sections of the code.

Instead of duplicating logic, refactor the code into reusable functions or classes. **DRY** (Don't Repeat Yourself) is a core principle of clean code.

Example: Avoiding Duplication

Duplicated Code:

cpp

```cpp
double calculatePriceWithTax(double price) {
    double tax = price * 0.1;
    return price + tax;
}

double calculateDiscountPrice(double price) {
    double discount = price * 0.2;
    return price - discount;
}
```

In this example, both functions calculate values based on a price. The tax and discount logic are similar, which means this code can be refactored to remove duplication.

Refactored Code:

cpp

```cpp
double calculateWithAdjustment(double price,
double percentage) {
    return price + (price * percentage);
}

double calculatePriceWithTax(double price) {
    return calculateWithAdjustment(price, 0.1);
}

double calculateDiscountPrice(double price) {
    return calculateWithAdjustment(price, -0.2);
}
```

By refactoring the shared logic into a helper function (`calculateWithAdjustment`), we eliminate duplication and make the code more maintainable.

3. Writing Self-Explanatory Code

Clean code should be **self-explanatory**. This means that, as much as possible, your code should convey its intent without requiring external explanations. This reduces the need for excessive comments and makes the code easier for other developers to understand.

To write self-explanatory code:

- **Use descriptive variable and function names**: A good name conveys the purpose of the variable or function without needing additional context.
- **Don't overcomplicate logic**: If the logic is too complex, break it down into smaller, more manageable pieces with meaningful names.

Example: Writing Self-Explanatory Code

Not Self-Explanatory:

cpp

```cpp
double a = 100;
double b = 0.2;
double c = a * b;
```

In the above code, the variables a, b, and c don't convey much meaning. A developer unfamiliar with the code would need to spend time figuring out what these variables represent.

Self-Explanatory:

cpp

```cpp
double totalPrice = 100;
double taxRate = 0.2;
```

```
double totalWithTax = totalPrice * taxRate;
```

In the refactored code, the variable names give clear indications of what the values represent, making the code easier to understand without additional comments.

The Importance of Readable Variable Names and Functions

The names you choose for **variables**, **functions**, and **classes** can make a big difference in how readable and maintainable your code is. Good names communicate the intent of the code and make the logic easier to follow.

1. Variable Naming

- Choose **descriptive names** that clearly indicate the purpose of the variable.
- Avoid single-letter names like x, y, and z unless they are commonly understood in context (e.g., loop counters).
- Use **meaningful names**: For example, use price instead of p or totalAmount instead of total.

Example:

Poor Variable Names:

35

```cpp
int a = 10;
int b = 20;
int c = a + b;
```

Good Variable Names:

```cpp
int itemPrice = 10;
int taxAmount = 20;
int totalAmount = itemPrice + taxAmount;
```

2. Function Naming

- Functions should be named using verbs to describe what they do.
- Ensure function names are **consistent** with their behavior.
- Avoid generic names like `process()` or `handle()` unless they describe a specific action.

Example:

Poor Function Name:

```cpp
void doStuff() {
    // Some complex logic
```

```
}
```

Good Function Name:

```cpp
cpp

void calculateTotalAmount() {
    // Some logic to calculate total
}
```

The second example is much more readable because the function name clearly indicates what it does.

Code Comments: When and How to Use Them Effectively

While the goal of clean code is to **avoid over-commenting**, there are situations where comments are necessary. However, comments should **explain why something is done**, not **what is done**, as the "what" should be clear from the code itself.

When to Use Comments:

- **Explain complex logic**: If a section of the code is complex or non-intuitive, a comment should clarify its purpose.

- **Document assumptions and decisions**: If there's a non-obvious reason for choosing a particular approach, document it in a comment.

Examples:

- **Good Comment**:

cpp

```
// Using a binary search algorithm for
faster lookup in sorted arrays
int result = binarySearch(sortedArray,
targetValue);
```

- **Bad Comment**:

cpp

```
// This line adds two numbers
int sum = a + b;
```

In the second example, the comment is unnecessary because the code is self-explanatory. If the logic requires a comment to be understood, it's a sign that the code might need to be refactored for clarity.

The Role of Consistent Formatting and Style Guides

Consistent **code formatting** and adherence to a **style guide** make it easier for multiple developers to work on the same project. A **style guide** ensures that the code follows a common structure and pattern, promoting readability and reducing confusion.

Key Formatting Practices:

- **Indentation**: Use consistent indentation (e.g., 4 spaces per level) to show the structure of the code.
- **Braces**: Place opening braces { on the same line as the control statement, unless your team follows a different convention.
- **Spaces**: Use spaces around operators and after commas for better readability.

Example:

Inconsistent Formatting:

cpp

```
int main() {int x=10; if (x>5) {x++;} return 0;}
```

Consistent Formatting:

39

cpp

```
int main() {
    int x = 10;
    if (x > 5) {
        x++;
    }
    return 0;
}
```

By following a consistent style guide, you ensure that your code is easy to read, maintain, and understand, even by developers who haven't seen it before.

Conclusion

The **fundamentals of clean code** involve focusing on clarity, simplicity, and maintainability. By adhering to principles like **simplicity, avoiding duplication**, and **writing self-explanatory code**, developers can write code that is not only functional but also easy to understand and maintain over time. **Readable variable names, function names**, and **code comments** are critical to making code approachable for other developers. Finally, adopting **consistent formatting and style guides** across a team helps foster collaboration and ensures that codebases remain manageable as they grow. Clean code is not just a set of rules—it's a mindset that improves both the quality of the code and the productivity of the team.

CHAPTER 3

CODE READABILITY: THE BACKBONE OF MAINTAINABLE CODE

Code readability is one of the most critical factors in writing **maintainable software**. No matter how well-optimized or feature-rich your code is, if it's difficult to read and understand, it becomes a nightmare to modify, extend, or debug. This chapter explores the importance of **structuring code for maximum readability**, focusing on aspects such as **indentation, spacing, line breaks**, and **whitespace**. It also provides guidelines on how to write **self-explanatory code** and offers real-world examples comparing poorly readable code with highly readable code.

Structuring Your Code for Maximum Readability

Code structure is the framework within which your program exists. A well-structured codebase improves **clarity, scalability**, and **debuggability**. Structuring your code properly helps both current and future developers understand its flow and logic at a glance.

1. Organize Code into Logical Blocks

To make code easy to follow, it should be organized into **logical blocks** or sections. Each block should represent a **single responsibility** (i.e., a specific task or function), and the flow of control should be easy to follow.

Best Practices:

- **Group related functions** together in classes or modules.
- Keep related **variables** and **constants** close to the code where they are used.
- Use **separation of concerns**: isolate different aspects of your program to make it more understandable.

Example: Well-Structured Code

cpp

```cpp
// Class to represent a bank account
class BankAccount {
private:
    double balance;
public:
    // Constructor to initialize the balance
    BankAccount(double    initial_balance)    :
balance(initial_balance) {}

    // Method to deposit money
    void deposit(double amount) {
```

43

```
        balance += amount;
    }

    // Method to withdraw money
    bool withdraw(double amount) {
        if (amount > balance) {
            return false;  // Insufficient funds
        }
        balance -= amount;
        return true;
    }

    // Get the current balance
    double getBalance() const {
        return balance;
    }
};
```

Here, the **BankAccount class** is structured in a way that logically groups related methods and variables. Each function has a **single responsibility**, and the flow is clear and easy to follow.

2. Use Appropriate Function and Variable Grouping

When writing functions, avoid cramming too many responsibilities into a single function. Keep functions short, each performing a **single task**. This also means grouping variables logically in functions and classes to improve readability.

Example: Clear Function Grouping

cpp

```cpp
void    calculateTotal(double    price,    double
taxRate) {
    double tax = price * taxRate;
    double total = price + tax;
    std::cout << "Total: " << total << std::endl;
}

void printReceipt(double price, double taxRate)
{
    calculateTotal(price, taxRate);   // Function
call for calculation
    // Additional code for printing receipt
}
```

In this example, **calculateTotal** handles the task of computing the total cost, while **printReceipt** handles receipt printing. Both tasks are separated into logically distinct functions, improving readability and focus.

Indentation, Spacing, and Line Breaks

Indentation, **spacing**, and **line breaks** help to visually separate code into blocks and make it more readable. Consistent formatting ensures that developers can instantly recognize where one section of code ends and another begins.

1. Proper Indentation

Use consistent **indentation** to indicate code hierarchy. In most modern coding environments, an indentation of **4 spaces** is the standard. Some teams or projects may use **tabs** instead, but the key is consistency throughout the project.

Example: Proper Indentation

cpp

```cpp
if (x > 0) {
    // Action when x is positive
    performPositiveAction();
} else {
    // Action when x is non-positive
    performNegativeAction();
}
```

This indentation clearly shows the structure of the if-else block and makes the logic easy to follow.

2. Spacing Between Code Elements

Using spaces effectively improves readability. Ensure there's adequate spacing between operators, arguments, and elements in your code.

Example: Proper Spacing

cpp

```cpp
int sum = a + b;   // Use spaces around operators
for clarity
```

3. Line Breaks to Separate Logical Units

Line breaks should be used to separate logically distinct blocks of code (e.g., functions, classes, or conditionals).

Example: Effective Line Breaks

cpp

```cpp
void initialize() {
    // Initialize variables
    int x = 10;
    int y = 20;
}

void process() {
    // Process data
    // Some logic here
}
```

By adding **line breaks** between distinct sections of the code, you make it easier for developers to discern the boundaries of different functionalities.

Use of Whitespace to Separate Concerns

Whitespace is often overlooked but plays a crucial role in separating concerns and enhancing code readability.

1. Logical Separation with Whitespace

Whitespace should be used to clearly **separate sections of code** that perform different tasks. For example, separate variable declarations, logic, and loops with blank lines.

Example: Logical Separation

cpp

```cpp
// Variable declarations
double price = 100;
double taxRate = 0.1;

// Calculate tax
double tax = price * taxRate;

// Print the result
std::cout << "Total price with tax: " << price +
tax << std::endl;
```

Here, blank lines are used to **visually separate** different concerns in the code: variable initialization, tax calculation, and output.

2. Whitespace for Formatting

Whitespace helps **align code** to enhance visual appeal and readability. For example, aligning function parameters, operators, or comments can make your code look more organized.

Example: Aligning Code for Clarity

cpp

```cpp
double   calculateTotal(double   price,   double
taxRate) {
    double tax   = price * taxRate;
    double total = price + tax;
    return total;
}
```

In this example, the alignment of `tax` and `total` enhances the **visual flow** of the code, making it easy to compare the values.

How to Write Self-Explanatory Code Without Comments

One of the hallmarks of clean code is the ability to **write self-explanatory code**. This means that, whenever possible, the **code itself** should explain its purpose and functionality, reducing the need for excessive comments.

1. Meaningful Variable and Function Names

By using **meaningful and descriptive names** for your variables and functions, the need for comments can be greatly reduced. The name should **describe** what the variable or function does.

Example: Self-Explanatory Code

cpp

```cpp
double calculateDiscount(double originalPrice,
double discountRate) {
    return originalPrice * (1 - discountRate);
}
```

In this example, the function name `calculateDiscount` clearly indicates what the function does, and the variable names `originalPrice` and `discountRate` clearly explain their roles, making comments unnecessary.

2. Break Complex Logic into Smaller Functions

When a function becomes complex, it's better to break it down into smaller, self-contained functions. Each smaller function should have a **clear purpose**, and the name should reflect that purpose.

Example: Breaking Down Complex Logic

cpp

```cpp
double calculateTax(double price) {
    return price * 0.1;
}

double calculateTotalPrice(double price) {
    double tax = calculateTax(price);
    return price + tax;
}
```

In this example, the code is more self-explanatory because each function handles a **specific task** and has a name that indicates its purpose.

Real-World Examples of Poorly Readable vs. Highly Readable Code

Poorly Readable Code Example

cpp

```cpp
double p1 = 100;   // Price of item 1
double p2 = 200;   // Price of item 2
double p3 = 300;   // Price of item 3
double p4 = 400;   // Price of item 4
double p5 = 500;   // Price of item 5

double t = 0;
```

```cpp
t = p1 + p2 + p3 + p4 + p5;   // Total of prices

double d = t * 0.1;   // Discount
double total = t - d;   // Final price
```

While this code is functional, it is **hard to follow**. The variable names (p1, p2, etc.) don't explain what they represent, and the total calculation process is spread out with little context.

Highly Readable Code Example

cpp

```cpp
double priceItem1 = 100;
double priceItem2 = 200;
double priceItem3 = 300;
double priceItem4 = 400;
double priceItem5 = 500;

double                totalPrice                =
calculateTotalPrice(priceItem1,      priceItem2,
priceItem3, priceItem4, priceItem5);
double discount = totalPrice * 0.1;
double finalPrice = totalPrice - discount;

std::cout << "The final price is: " << finalPrice
<< std::endl;
```

```
double calculateTotalPrice(double item1, double
item2, double item3, double item4, double item5)
{
    return item1 + item2 + item3 + item4 + item5;
}
```

In this example, the code is much **easier to follow**. The variable names clearly represent the prices of individual items, and the function `calculateTotalPrice` encapsulates the logic for adding the prices, making the code more **modular** and **self-explanatory**.

Conclusion

Code readability is the backbone of maintainable and scalable software. Structuring your code logically, adhering to consistent indentation and spacing practices, and writing self-explanatory code reduces the cognitive load on developers. When code is easy to read, understand, and modify, it's easier to maintain and scale over time. By following these **best practices** for readability, you can significantly improve the quality and longevity of your code. In the next chapter, we'll dive deeper into **variable naming** and **function design**, focusing on best practices that make code even more intuitive and efficient.

CHAPTER 4

FUNCTIONS: THE BUILDING BLOCKS OF CLEAN CODE

Functions are the **building blocks of clean code**. They allow us to break down complex problems into smaller, manageable pieces. A well-written function can make code much easier to understand, maintain, and extend. In this chapter, we will cover the **principles for writing clean functions**, the importance of keeping functions **small and focused**, proper **function naming conventions**, the need to **avoid side effects**, and how to decide when to **split or combine functions**. With real-world examples, we will explore the best practices for writing functions that contribute to clean, maintainable code.

Principles for Writing Clean Functions

Writing clean functions starts with understanding the purpose of a function: to perform a specific task. Clean functions should be easy to understand, focused on a single responsibility, and not over-complicated. Below are the core principles that guide clean function design:

1. Single Responsibility

A function should ideally perform only **one task**. By adhering to the **Single Responsibility Principle (SRP)**, each function can be understood and tested independently, making it easier to maintain and extend over time.

- **Don't try to do everything in one function**. If a function is trying to accomplish multiple tasks, it becomes harder to understand, test, and maintain.

Example: Single Responsibility

cpp

```cpp
// Bad: Function does too much
void processOrder(int orderId, double price,
std::string customerEmail) {
    // Calculate total price
    double totalPrice = price + (price * 0.1);
// Adding tax

    // Send confirmation email
    sendConfirmationEmail(customerEmail,
totalPrice);

    // Store order in the database
    storeOrderInDatabase(orderId, totalPrice,
customerEmail);
}
```

```
// Good: Functions with single responsibilities
void calculateTotalPrice(double price) {
    return price + (price * 0.1);  // Adding tax
}

void            sendConfirmationEmail(std::string
customerEmail, double totalPrice) {
    // Send email logic
}

void storeOrderInDatabase(int  orderId,  double
totalPrice, std::string customerEmail) {
    // Store order logic
}
```

In the **bad example**, the `processOrder` function does everything—calculating the price, sending an email, and saving the order. Each of these tasks should be separated into its own function. The **good example** breaks the responsibilities into **three distinct functions**, each focusing on a single task.

---

2. Keep Functions Small

A function should be **small enough** that it can be understood at a glance. If a function exceeds a few lines, it's a good sign that it's doing too much. Aim for **functions that can be scanned easily**— around **10-15 lines of code** is usually a good rule of thumb.

- **Small functions** are easier to read and understand, reducing the cognitive load required to grasp their purpose.
- Small functions also tend to be easier to test because they have fewer dependencies and focus on one task.

Example: Large vs. Small Functions

cpp

```cpp
// Bad: Large function that does too much
void        processCustomerOrder(int        orderId,
std::string customerEmail) {
    // Fetch order details from the database
    // Validate order details
    // Calculate discounts and taxes
    // Apply loyalty points
    // Generate invoice
    // Send email confirmation
    // Log order details
}


// Good: Small, focused functions
void fetchOrderDetails(int orderId) {
    // Fetch order details
}

void calculateDiscount(double price) {
    // Calculate discount
}
```

```
void generateInvoice(int orderId) {
    // Generate invoice
}

void sendEmailConfirmation(std::string email) {
    // Send email
}
```

In the **bad example**, the function `processCustomerOrder` is doing everything, making it difficult to follow and maintain. By **breaking it down into smaller, focused functions**, as shown in the **good example**, each function has one clear responsibility, making the code much more **manageable** and **maintainable**.

---

3. Proper Function Naming Conventions

A function name should describe **what it does** in a clear and concise manner. The name should ideally follow a **verb-noun** convention (e.g., `calculateTotal`, `sendEmail`, `fetchData`), making it intuitive for others to understand the function's purpose without needing to inspect the function body.

Naming Tips:

- Use **descriptive verbs** that clearly communicate the function's action.

- Avoid generic names like `doStuff` or `processData`. These names don't tell us what the function is really doing.
- For functions that return a boolean, use prefixes like `is`, `has`, or `can` (e.g., `isValid()`, `hasPermission()`, `canProcess()`).

Example: Descriptive Function Names

cpp

```cpp
// Bad: Ambiguous function name
void processData(int data) {
    // Processes data in an unknown way
}


// Good: Descriptive function name
void saveDataToDatabase(int data) {
    // Saves data to a database
}
```

The second example, with the function name `saveDataToDatabase`, is far more descriptive and makes it clear exactly what the function does.

4. The Importance of Avoiding Side Effects

A **side effect** is any change to the state of the system that is **not directly related to the function's output**. Functions with side effects can cause unexpected behavior and make debugging difficult. Functions should ideally be **pure**—meaning they should only return a result based on their inputs, without altering any state outside of the function.

Avoid functions that:

- Modify global variables or external states.
- Perform I/O operations (like writing to a file or printing to the console) unless absolutely necessary.

Example: Avoiding Side Effects

cpp

```cpp
// Bad: Function with side effects (modifying global state)
int counter = 0;

void incrementCounter() {
    counter++;  // Side effect: modifying global variable
}

// Good: Pure function with no side effects
int incrementCounter(int counter) {
```

```
    return counter + 1;   // Returns a new value
without modifying external state
}
```

In the **bad example**, the function `incrementCounter` changes the value of a global variable `counter`, which is a side effect that can cause unpredictable behavior in other parts of the program. The **good example** avoids this by returning a new value without modifying any external state.

When to Split or Combine Functions: Real-World Examples

One of the most important aspects of function design is knowing when to **split a function** into smaller pieces and when to **combine multiple functions** into one.

1. When to Split a Function

You should split a function into smaller functions when:

- The function is too **large** or **complex**.
- The function is trying to handle **multiple responsibilities**.

Example: Splitting a Function

cpp

```
// Bad: Function is too large
void generateReport(int startDate, int endDate)
{
    // Fetch data from database
    // Process data
    // Generate PDF
    // Send email with report
}

// Good: Splitting into smaller functions
void fetchDataFromDatabase(int startDate, int
endDate) {
    // Fetch data logic
}

void processData() {
    // Process data logic
}

void generatePDF() {
    // PDF generation logic
}

void sendEmail() {
    // Email sending logic
}
```

In this example, the original function `generateReport` is doing too much. By splitting it into smaller functions with **single responsibilities**, the code becomes more modular and easier to maintain.

2. When to Combine Functions

You should combine functions when:

- The functions perform similar tasks or represent the same concept.
- Combining them leads to **greater clarity** and **reduces duplication**.

Example: Combining Functions

cpp

```cpp
// Bad: Separate functions for similar tasks
void printInvoice(int orderId) {
    // Logic to print invoice
}

void printReceipt(int orderId) {
    // Logic to print receipt
}

// Good: Combine into a single function
void printDocument(int orderId, std::string documentType) {
```

```
if (documentType == "Invoice") {
    // Logic to print invoice
} else if (documentType == "Receipt") {
    // Logic to print receipt
}
}
```

In this case, instead of having two separate functions `printInvoice` and `printReceipt`, we combine them into one function `printDocument`, which makes the code easier to maintain and less redundant.

Conclusion

Functions are the **building blocks of clean code**. By adhering to the principles of **single responsibility**, keeping functions **small and focused**, using **proper naming conventions**, and avoiding **side effects**, you can create functions that are **easy to read**, **maintain**, and **extend**. Additionally, knowing when to **split** or **combine** functions based on their complexity and responsibility will help you build a clean, modular codebase.

Clean functions are an essential part of writing maintainable code. They not only improve readability but also make it easier to debug, test, and extend your application. As you continue developing software, remember that the effort you put into writing clean, concise, and well-organized functions will pay off in the long run, making your projects more manageable and scalable.

CHAPTER 5

VARIABLES AND CONSTANTS: NAMING AND USAGE BEST PRACTICES

In this chapter, we will dive into the best practices for naming and using **variables** and **constants** in a way that promotes readability, maintainability, and clarity. A key component of clean code is using **meaningful names** for variables and constants, as well as avoiding hard-coded values and "magic numbers" that obscure the intent of your code. By adhering to these best practices, you can ensure your code is intuitive, easy to modify, and scalable.

Meaningful Variable Names: How to Choose Them

Choosing the right names for your variables is one of the most important aspects of writing clean code. A variable's name should clearly indicate its purpose in the program. This makes your code easier to read and maintain, reducing the cognitive load on anyone who needs to understand it.

1. Descriptive and Intent-Revealing Names

A good variable name should **reveal its purpose**. For example, if a variable stores the total price of items, naming it `totalPrice` is much clearer than naming it `t` or `price1`. Avoid using short, non-descriptive names like `a`, `x`, or `temp`, unless they are loop counters or other short-lived variables with an obvious context.

Good Examples:

- `totalAmount, totalPrice, userAge`
- `itemQuantity,` `discountPercentage, employeeSalary`

Bad Examples:

- `a, x, temp`
- `var1, val, num`

2. Use Consistent Naming Conventions

Adhering to a consistent naming convention is critical, particularly when working in teams. This helps developers know what to expect when they see a variable name. For instance, you might use **camelCase** for variables (`itemQuantity`, `totalPrice`), and **PascalCase** for classes (`InvoiceProcessor, UserManager`).

67

3. Avoid Unnecessary Abbreviations

While abbreviations might seem like a shortcut, they often lead to confusion. For instance, `amt` could be ambiguous—does it represent an amount, an amplitude, or something else? Use full, descriptive words whenever possible.

Good Example:

- `totalAmount, itemPrice, userEmail`

Bad Example:

- `amt, itmQty, usrEmail`

4. Meaningful Context

Variable names should reflect not only the data they hold but also the **context** of their use. For example, instead of `counter` for a variable that tracks the number of items in a shopping cart, use `shoppingCartItemCount`. This provides more context and clarifies its purpose.

Example: Adding Context

cpp

```
int counter;    // Ambiguous
int shoppingCartItemCount;  // Clear and context-
rich
```

The Role of Constants and Why They Matter

Constants are values that do not change throughout the execution of a program. They are crucial for **improving code readability** and **maintaining consistency**. Instead of hard-coding a value multiple times, you can define it as a constant, making the code easier to change and reducing the risk of errors.

1. Using Constants for Fixed Values

By using constants, you prevent accidental changes to values that are meant to remain fixed, such as mathematical constants, configuration values, or system-specific limits.

Example:

cpp

```cpp
const double PI = 3.14159;
const int MAX_USERS = 100;
```

In this example, PI and MAX_USERS are constants, and using them ensures that these values cannot be altered accidentally.

69

2. Why Constants Matter:

- **Avoids magic numbers**: Instead of embedding values like `3.14159` or `100` throughout your code, you use named constants that explain their purpose.
- **Easy to update**: If you need to change a value (e.g., `MAX_USERS`), you only need to update it in one place.
- **Improves maintainability**: Future developers (or even future you) will understand the role of constants when reading the code.

Avoiding Magic Numbers and Hard-Coded Values

A **magic number** is a literal value that appears in the code without explanation. For example, if your code has `x = 5;`, the number 5 is a magic number unless its purpose is immediately obvious. Using magic numbers makes the code harder to maintain and understand.

1. Why Magic Numbers are Problematic

- **Lack of context**: Without any indication of what the value represents, it's hard to know why it's used in a specific context.

- **Difficulty in maintenance**: If the value needs to change, you might miss one instance of it, leading to inconsistent behavior or errors.

Example of Magic Numbers:

cpp

```
double totalCost = price * 0.2;   // What is 0.2?
Tax? Discount?
```

In the above example, it's unclear whether 0.2 represents a tax rate, a discount, or some other value.

2. How to Avoid Magic Numbers

- **Use constants**: Replace magic numbers with constants that explain their purpose.
- **Use enums for sets of related values**: When you have a set of fixed options (e.g., months, states), use an enum.

Refactored Code: Avoiding Magic Numbers

cpp

```
const double TAX_RATE = 0.2;   // Clearly named
constant for tax rate
double totalCost = price * TAX_RATE;
```

When to Use Constants, Enums, and Configuration Files

Knowing when and where to define constants, enums, and configuration files is key to writing maintainable code. Let's look at the best scenarios for using each.

1. Constants

Use **constants** for values that do not change throughout the program, such as:

- Fixed mathematical values (e.g., PI).
- Limits or thresholds (e.g., MAX_USERS).
- Units of measure (e.g., SECONDS_IN_A_MINUTE).

Example:

cpp

```
const int SECONDS_IN_A_MINUTE = 60;
const double TAX_RATE = 0.2;
```

2. Enums

Use **enums** when you have a set of predefined, related constants. Enums provide a more readable way to handle sets of related values, especially when these values are used multiple times throughout the code.

Example:

```
cpp
```

```cpp
enum class OrderStatus {
    Pending,
    Shipped,
    Delivered,
    Cancelled
};


OrderStatus status = OrderStatus::Shipped;
```

Enums help make the code more self-explanatory by using meaningful names for different values.

3. Configuration Files

If a value needs to be **modifiable by a user** or may change across different environments (e.g., production, testing), it's best to store that value in a **configuration file** rather than hard-coding it into the program.

Example:

Instead of hard-coding the database connection string, store it in a configuration file like `config.json`:

```
json
```

```
{
    "db_connection_string":
"server=localhost;uid=root;pwd=secret;"
}
```

The application can then load this value at runtime, making it easier to modify without changing the codebase.

Real-World Examples of Poor Variable Names vs. Good Variable Names

To understand the importance of meaningful variable names, let's compare some **poor variable names** with **good ones** in real-world scenarios.

Example 1: Variable Names in a Calculation Function

cpp

```
// Bad variable names
double x = 100;
double y = 200;
double z = x + y;    // What do x, y, and z
represent?

// Good variable names
double itemPrice = 100;
double taxAmount = 200;
```

74

```cpp
double totalPrice = itemPrice + taxAmount;   //
Clear and descriptive
```

In this example, the bad variable names x, y, and z lack any meaningful context. On the other hand, the good variable names (itemPrice, taxAmount, totalPrice) clearly explain the role of each variable, making the code **easier to understand** and **maintain**.

Example 2: Descriptive Names in a Loop

cpp

```cpp
// Bad variable names in a loop
for (int i = 0; i < n; i++) {
    arr[i] = i * 2;
}

// Good variable names in a loop
for (int index = 0; index < arrayLength; index++)
{
    array[index] = index * 2;
}
```

In the **bad example**, the loop variable i and the array arr don't provide enough context, while in the **good example**, index and arrayLength are more descriptive, making it clear what the loop is doing.

Conclusion

In this chapter, we've explored best practices for naming and using **variables** and **constants**. By choosing **meaningful variable names**, **avoiding magic numbers**, and using **constants**, **enums**, and **configuration files** where appropriate, you make your code **cleaner**, **more readable**, and **easier to maintain**. Naming conventions are essential for conveying intent and making your code understandable to other developers.

Through real-world examples, we've demonstrated how poor variable names can make code confusing and how well-chosen names can enhance clarity and maintainability. By following these practices, you'll be able to write code that is not only functional but also easy to understand, modify, and extend—essential qualities of clean, maintainable code.

CHAPTER 6

CLASSES AND OBJECTS: DESIGNING WITH PURPOSE

Object-Oriented Programming (OOP) is a powerful paradigm for designing clean, maintainable, and scalable software. In this chapter, we will explore how to design **classes and objects** with purpose to ensure they are cohesive, reusable, and maintainable. We'll discuss the core **Object-Oriented principles** that help you write clean code, the decision-making process behind **creating new classes vs. reusing existing ones**, and how to **encapsulate behavior and data** effectively. We'll also explore the importance of creating **cohesive** and **loosely coupled** classes to improve maintainability and flexibility in your codebase.

Object-Oriented Principles for Writing Clean Code

Object-Oriented Programming is built on the foundation of a few key principles, and applying these principles can help you write clean, organized, and maintainable code. Let's briefly review these principles:

1. Encapsulation

Encapsulation refers to the concept of bundling data (attributes) and the methods that operate on that data into a single unit, i.e., a **class**. This principle helps hide the internal workings of a class from the outside world, exposing only necessary functionality.

- **Encapsulation helps** by restricting direct access to certain attributes and ensuring that they can only be modified through well-defined methods, leading to more **controlled and predictable behavior**.

Example: Encapsulating an Account's Balance

cpp

```
class BankAccount {
private:
    double balance;   // Balance is private and
cannot be directly accessed
public:
    BankAccount(double    initialBalance)    :
balance(initialBalance) {}

    // Public method to get balance
    double getBalance() const {
        return balance;
    }

    // Public method to deposit funds
```

```
void deposit(double amount) {
    if (amount > 0) {
        balance += amount;
    }
}

// Public method to withdraw funds
bool withdraw(double amount) {
    if (amount > 0 && amount <= balance) {
        balance -= amount;
        return true;
    }
    return false;
}
};
```

In this example, **balance** is **encapsulated** within the `BankAccount` class, and external code cannot access or modify it directly. The **deposit** and **withdraw** methods are the only ways to modify the balance, which ensures that the class behaves consistently.

2. Inheritance

Inheritance allows a class to inherit attributes and behaviors (methods) from another class. It promotes **code reuse** and enables creating specialized classes based on a more general one.

- Inheritance allows us to build a hierarchy of classes, improving **organization** and **extensibility**.

3. Polymorphism

Polymorphism allows objects of different types to be treated as objects of a common base type. The most common form is **method overriding**, where subclasses provide specific implementations of methods that are defined in a parent class.

- Polymorphism makes code more flexible and extensible, allowing you to use **base class references** or **pointers** to refer to objects of derived classes.

When to Create a New Class vs. When to Use Existing Ones

In object-oriented design, deciding when to create a new class or reuse an existing one is crucial for maintaining a clean and scalable codebase. Here are some guidelines for making that decision:

1. When to Create a New Class

- **When you need a distinct entity**: If you are modeling a distinct real-world object, create a class. For example, a

Car class, a Customer class, or a Product class should each be modeled as their own entities.

- **When functionality is unrelated to existing classes**: If the behavior or attributes of the entity do not fit within the scope of an existing class, it's time to create a new class.

Example:

If you're developing an e-commerce system and need to represent orders, creating a new Order class makes sense because it represents a separate concept with its own attributes and behavior.

cpp

```cpp
class Order {
private:
    int orderId;
    double orderTotal;
public:
    Order(int id, double total) : orderId(id),
orderTotal(total) {}

    void updateOrderTotal(double total) {
        orderTotal = total;
    }

    double getOrderTotal() const {
        return orderTotal;
    }
```

```
};
```

2. When to Use Existing Classes

- **When the behavior is already modeled**: If the functionality or behavior you want to add is already covered by an existing class, use that class instead of creating a new one. For instance, a `Payment` class might already handle the logic for processing payments, so you can reuse it rather than creating a new class.
- **When you're extending an existing class**: In cases where you need to add new features to an existing entity, you should consider using inheritance to extend the existing class instead of creating a new one.

Example:

If you have a `Person` class, and you need to create specific types of people (like `Employee` or `Student`), it makes sense to extend `Person` rather than creating entirely new classes for each.

cpp

```cpp
class Employee : public Person {
private:
    double salary;
public:
    Employee(std::string name, double salary) :
Person(name), salary(salary) {}
```

```cpp
double getSalary() const {
    return salary;
}
};
```

In this case, the `Employee` class extends `Person` and **reuses** its functionality, only adding specific behavior related to salary.

Using Classes to Encapsulate Behavior and Data

A core tenet of OOP is **encapsulation**, which involves bundling **data** (attributes) and **behavior** (methods) together in a class. This ensures that an object can control how its data is accessed and modified, improving **security**, **maintainability**, and **flexibility**.

- **Behavior** refers to what an object can do (its **methods**).
- **Data** refers to the information an object holds (its **attributes**).

By encapsulating behavior and data together, a class can ensure that its internal state is always in a valid state and that only meaningful operations are allowed.

Example: Class with Encapsulated Data and Behavior

cpp

```cpp
class Rectangle {
private:
    double width, height;

public:
    // Constructor to initialize the rectangle
dimensions
    Rectangle(double w, double h) : width(w),
height(h) {}

    // Public methods to interact with the
rectangle
    double area() const {
        return width * height;
    }

    double perimeter() const {
        return 2 * (width + height);
    }

    void setDimensions(double w, double h) {
        if (w > 0 && h > 0) {
            width = w;
            height = h;
        }
    }
};
```

In this example, the `Rectangle` class encapsulates both the **data** (width and height) and the **behavior** (calculating the area and perimeter, setting dimensions). This ensures that all rectangle-related functionality is logically grouped together and that the rectangle's internal state remains consistent.

The Importance of Cohesive and Loosely Coupled Classes

Two key design principles for writing clean object-oriented code are **cohesion** and **coupling**:

1. Cohesion

- **Cohesion** refers to how closely related the methods and data of a class are. A highly cohesive class focuses on a single responsibility and has methods that are strongly related to each other.
- High cohesion leads to **easier maintainability** because the class's behavior and data are logically grouped.

Example:

A `Customer` class that handles only customer-related behaviors (e.g., storing and retrieving customer information) exhibits high cohesion.

85

```cpp
cpp

class Customer {
private:
    std::string name;
    std::string email;
public:
    Customer(std::string            customerName,
std::string customerEmail) : name(customerName),
email(customerEmail) {}

    std::string getName() const {
        return name;
    }

    std::string getEmail() const {
        return email;
    }

    void updateEmail(std::string newEmail) {
        email = newEmail;
    }
};
```

2. Loose Coupling

- **Coupling** refers to how dependent one class is on another. **Loosely coupled classes** are those that are not overly dependent on each other and can function independently, making the system more flexible and easier to change.

86

- **Loose coupling** promotes **modularity**, which makes code easier to maintain and scale.

Example: Loose Coupling

If the Order class interacts with a payment system, instead of tightly coupling the Order class to a specific payment provider, you can abstract the payment method via interfaces or abstract classes.

cpp

```cpp
class PaymentProcessor {
public:
    virtual void processPayment(double amount) =
0;
};

class PayPalProcessor : public PaymentProcessor
{
public:
    void processPayment(double amount) override
{
        // PayPal payment processing logic
    }
};

class Order {
private:
```

```
    PaymentProcessor*    paymentProcessor;        //
Interface dependency
public:
    Order(PaymentProcessor*    processor)    :
paymentProcessor(processor) {}

    void makePayment(double amount) {
        paymentProcessor-
>processPayment(amount);
    }
};
```

In this example, `Order` is **loosely coupled** to the actual payment implementation. You can easily swap out `PayPalProcessor` for any other `PaymentProcessor` implementation (like `CreditCardProcessor`) without modifying the `Order` class. This improves **flexibility** and **maintainability**.

Real-World Examples of Class Design in Software Applications

1. Banking System

In a **banking system**, classes can represent different aspects like **accounts**, **transactions**, and **customers**. Each class should be responsible for a distinct aspect of the domain.

```cpp
cpp

class BankAccount {
private:
    double balance;
public:
    BankAccount(double    initialBalance)    :
balance(initialBalance) {}

    void deposit(double amount) {
        balance += amount;
    }

    void withdraw(double amount) {
        if (amount <= balance) {
            balance -= amount;
        }
    }

    double getBalance() const {
        return balance;
    }
};

class Transaction {
private:
    BankAccount* account;
    double amount;
public:
```

```cpp
    Transaction(BankAccount* acc, double amt) :
account(acc), amount(amt) {}

    void executeTransaction() {
        account->withdraw(amount);
    }
};
```

Here, the **BankAccount** class is cohesive, handling only account-related behaviors, while the **Transaction** class handles transaction-specific logic.

2. E-commerce Platform

In an **e-commerce platform**, different objects might represent **orders**, **products**, **inventory**, and **customers**. Each class will encapsulate the related behavior and data.

cpp

```cpp
class Product {
private:
    std::string name;
    double price;
public:
    Product(std::string productName, double
productPrice)        :        name(productName),
price(productPrice) {}
```

90

```
double getPrice() const {
    return price;
}

std::string getName() const {
    return name;
}
};
```

The **Product** class is simple and cohesive, focusing only on product-related data and behavior, making it easy to extend and maintain.

Conclusion

Designing classes and objects with purpose is fundamental to writing clean, maintainable software. By following **Object-Oriented principles** such as **encapsulation, inheritance**, and **polymorphism**, you can write code that is flexible, easy to modify, and easy to understand. Whether deciding when to create a new class, how to **encapsulate behavior and data**, or how to maintain **cohesion** and **loose coupling**, each decision should be guided by the goal of writing clear, efficient, and scalable code.

Through real-world examples of class design, we've seen how applying these principles results in more **organized, modular**, and **maintainable** software. As you continue to write object-oriented code, remember that the purpose of every class is to fulfill a specific responsibility, and the design of that class should reflect this purpose.

CHAPTER 7

SOLID PRINCIPLES: WRITING SCALABLE OBJECT-ORIENTED CODE

In object-oriented programming, creating software that is both **scalable** and **maintainable** is essential for long-term success. One of the most powerful ways to achieve this is by applying the **SOLID principles**. These principles—**Single Responsibility Principle (SRP), Open/Closed Principle (OCP), Liskov Substitution Principle (LSP), Interface Segregation Principle (ISP)**, and **Dependency Inversion Principle (DIP)**—form the foundation of writing clean, modular, and flexible code. This chapter introduces each SOLID principle in detail, provides real-world case studies of these principles in practice, and discusses how to apply SOLID to legacy systems.

Introduction to SOLID Principles

The **SOLID principles** were introduced by **Robert C. Martin (Uncle Bob)** as a set of five design principles to help software developers create **highly maintainable, scalable**, and **robust** object-oriented systems. By adhering to these principles, you can reduce the likelihood of introducing bugs, improve code clarity, and make it easier to add new features without breaking existing functionality.

Each principle is aimed at achieving a specific goal in software design:

1. **Single Responsibility Principle (SRP)**
2. **Open/Closed Principle (OCP)**
3. **Liskov Substitution Principle (LSP)**
4. **Interface Segregation Principle (ISP)**
5. **Dependency Inversion Principle (DIP)**

Let's take a deep dive into each principle and explore how they can be applied to ensure clean, maintainable, and scalable code.

Single Responsibility Principle (SRP)

The **Single Responsibility Principle (SRP)** states that **a class should have only one reason to change**. This means that a class should only be responsible for one piece of functionality and should not be tasked with multiple, unrelated responsibilities. When a class has multiple responsibilities, changes to one responsibility can affect other parts of the class, making the code harder to understand, maintain, and test.

94

Example: Applying SRP

cpp

```cpp
// Bad: A class with multiple responsibilities
class OrderProcessor {
public:
    void processOrder(Order order) {
        // Process order
        // Save order to database
        // Send order confirmation email
    }
};


// Good: Split responsibilities into separate
classes
class OrderProcessor {
public:
    void processOrder(Order order) {
        // Process order logic
    }
};


class OrderSaver {
public:
    void saveToDatabase(Order order) {
        // Save order to database logic
    }
};
```

```cpp
class OrderConfirmationEmailer {
public:
    void sendEmail(Order order) {
        // Send confirmation email logic
    }
};
```

In the **bad example**, the `OrderProcessor` class has multiple responsibilities: processing the order, saving it to the database, and sending a confirmation email. In the **good example**, we separate these responsibilities into **distinct classes**: `OrderProcessor`, `OrderSaver`, and `OrderConfirmationEmailer`, each responsible for a single task.

Open/Closed Principle (OCP)

The **Open/Closed Principle (OCP)** asserts that **software entities (classes, modules, functions, etc.) should be open for extension but closed for modification**. This means that once a class or module is written, it should be easy to add new functionality without altering the existing code. This is typically achieved by using abstraction and inheritance, allowing for new behavior to be added through extensions, rather than modifying the core logic.

Example: Applying OCP

cpp

```cpp
// Bad: Modifying existing class to add new
functionality
class Shape {
public:
    virtual double calculateArea() = 0;
};


class Rectangle : public Shape {
public:
    double calculateArea() override {
        // Calculate area of rectangle
        return length * width;
    }
};


class Circle : public Shape {
public:
    double calculateArea() override {
        // Calculate area of circle
        return radius * radius * 3.14;
    }
};


// Adding new functionality by modifying existing
classes breaks OCP

// Good: Open for extension but closed for
modification
```

```cpp
class Shape {
public:
    virtual double calculateArea() = 0;
};


class Rectangle : public Shape {
public:
    double calculateArea() override {
        return length * width;
    }
};


class Circle : public Shape {
public:
    double calculateArea() override {
        return radius * radius * 3.14;
    }
};


// We can extend the code without modifying
existing functionality:
class Triangle : public Shape {
public:
    double calculateArea() override {
        return 0.5 * base * height;
    }
};
```

In the **bad example**, every time we need to add a new shape, we modify the existing Shape class and its subclasses. This violates OCP. In the **good example**, we extend the Shape class by adding new subclasses, such as Triangle, without changing the existing code, thereby adhering to OCP.

Liskov Substitution Principle (LSP)

The **Liskov Substitution Principle (LSP)** asserts that **objects of a subclass should be substitutable for objects of the parent class** without altering the correctness of the program. In other words, if a class B is a subclass of class A, you should be able to replace A with B without affecting the functionality of the program.

Example: Applying LSP

cpp

```cpp
// Bad: Violating LSP
class Bird {
public:
    virtual void fly() {
        // Default fly behavior
    }
};
```

```
class Ostrich : public Bird {
public:
    void fly() override {
        // Ostrich cannot fly, so this is not a
valid implementation
    }
};


// Good: Refactor to adhere to LSP
class Bird {
public:
    virtual void move() = 0;
};


class Sparrow : public Bird {
public:
    void move() override {
        // Sparrow flies
    }
};


class Ostrich : public Bird {
public:
    void move() override {
        // Ostrich walks
    }
};
```

In the **bad example**, the `Ostrich` class violates LSP because it cannot fly, yet we are trying to force it to implement the `fly` method. In the **good example**, we refactor the design so that both `Sparrow` and `Ostrich` inherit from `Bird` and implement their own behavior for `move`, adhering to LSP.

Interface Segregation Principle (ISP)

The **Interface Segregation Principle (ISP)** states that **clients should not be forced to depend on interfaces they do not use**. This principle encourages the use of smaller, more focused interfaces instead of large, monolithic ones. If a class implements an interface that has methods it doesn't need, it is violating ISP.

Example: Applying ISP

cpp

```cpp
// Bad: A large interface with methods that some
classes don't use
class Worker {
public:
    virtual void work() = 0;
    virtual void eat() = 0;
};

class Robot : public Worker {
```

```
public:
    void work() override {
        // Perform robotic work
    }
    void eat() override {
        // Robots don't eat, so this method
doesn't make sense
    }
};

// Good: Segregated interfaces
class Workable {
public:
    virtual void work() = 0;
};

class Eatable {
public:
    virtual void eat() = 0;
};

class Robot : public Workable {
public:
    void work() override {
        // Perform robotic work
    }
};

class Human : public Workable, public Eatable {
```

```
public:
    void work() override {
        // Human work logic
    }
    void eat() override {
        // Human eat logic
    }
};
```

In the **bad example**, the `Robot` class is forced to implement the `eat` method, even though it doesn't make sense for a robot. In the **good example**, the interface is **segregated** into `Workable` and `Eatable`, and the `Robot` class only implements the `Workable` interface, adhering to ISP.

Dependency Inversion Principle (DIP)

The **Dependency Inversion Principle (DIP)** suggests that **high-level modules should not depend on low-level modules. Both should depend on abstractions**. Additionally, **abstractions should not depend on details. Details should depend on abstractions**. This principle advocates for decoupling classes from their dependencies, which makes the system easier to modify and extend.

Example: Applying DIP

cpp

```cpp
// Bad: High-level module depends directly on
low-level module
class LightBulb {
public:
    void turnOn() {
        // Turn on light bulb
    }
    void turnOff() {
        // Turn off light bulb
    }
};

class Switch {
private:
    LightBulb bulb;
public:
    void operate() {
        bulb.turnOn();      // Switch directly
controls LightBulb
    }
};

// Good: Both high-level and low-level modules
depend on abstractions
class Switchable {
public:
```

104

```
    virtual void turnOn() = 0;
    virtual void turnOff() = 0;
};


class LightBulb : public Switchable {
public:
    void turnOn() override {
        // Turn on light bulb
    }
    void turnOff() override {
        // Turn off light bulb
    }
};


class Switch {
private:
    Switchable* device;
public:
    Switch(Switchable* dev) : device(dev) {}
    void operate() {
        device->turnOn();   // Switch depends on
abstraction (Switchable)
    }
};
```

In the **bad example**, the Switch class directly depends on the LightBulb class, making it difficult to change the light source or add new devices. In the **good example**, both Switch and

`LightBulb` depend on the `Switchable` abstraction, adhering to DIP and making the code more flexible.

Real-World Case Studies of SOLID in Practice

1. Case Study: E-commerce System

In a real-world e-commerce system, SOLID principles can help structure the codebase so that it's scalable and easy to maintain:

- **SRP**: The `OrderProcessor` class handles only order-related logic, while the `PaymentProcessor` handles payment processing.
- **OCP**: Adding a new payment method, like `PayPal`, does not require modifying the `PaymentProcessor`; we just add a new class implementing the `PaymentMethod` interface.
- **LSP**: A `CreditCardPayment` class can be substituted with a `PayPalPayment` class without affecting the payment processing logic.
- **ISP**: Instead of one large `PaymentProcessor` interface, we have separate interfaces for `Refundable` and `Chargeable`.

106

- **DIP**: The `PaymentService` class depends on an abstraction like `PaymentGateway`, not on a specific implementation like `PayPalGateway`.

How to Implement SOLID in Legacy Systems

Implementing SOLID in legacy systems can be challenging but is essential for making the system more maintainable and scalable. Here are some strategies for introducing SOLID principles into legacy code:

1. **Refactor One Class at a Time**: Start by applying SRP, breaking large, monolithic classes into smaller, focused classes.
2. **Introduce Interfaces and Abstractions**: Use interfaces and abstractions to decouple classes and reduce direct dependencies (DIP).
3. **Test and Apply Gradually**: Introduce each principle gradually while ensuring existing functionality is preserved through unit tests.
4. **Leverage Refactoring Techniques**: Use refactoring tools and techniques to avoid introducing bugs while applying SOLID principles to existing code.

Conclusion

The **SOLID principles** provide a solid foundation for designing clean, maintainable, and scalable object-oriented software. By adhering to **SRP**, **OCP**, **LSP**, **ISP**, and **DIP**, you ensure that your classes are cohesive, flexible, and easy to extend. These principles not only help write better software but also make it easier to collaborate with others, adapt to new requirements, and scale over time.

Applying SOLID to legacy systems can be a gradual process, but it's a worthwhile investment that significantly improves the quality and longevity of your software. Keep these principles in mind as you design your classes and interfaces, and your code will be more adaptable and easier to maintain in the long run.

CHAPTER 8

AVOIDING CODE SMELLS

In the process of software development, **"code smells"** refer to certain patterns or characteristics in the code that indicate potential problems, even if the code is technically functional. These smells are usually signs that the code is not **maintainable, scalable**, or **readable** and may need to be refactored. While a code smell doesn't necessarily mean a bug, it often indicates that something could be improved. In this chapter, we will explore what code smells are, identify common examples, and discuss techniques for refactoring them into clean, maintainable code.

What Are Code Smells?

A **code smell** is a metaphorical term used to describe certain aspects of the code that are indicative of a deeper problem. It may not necessarily cause errors or bugs, but it can make the codebase more difficult to understand, maintain, or extend. These "smells" often arise when the code is too complex, overly coupled, or poorly structured.

In simple terms, code smells are like signs of **bad hygiene** in your code. They don't directly indicate that something is broken but suggest that there's a **problem waiting to happen**—like bugs, inefficiencies, or difficulty in making changes to the system.

Why Do Code Smells Matter?

- **Increased Complexity**: Code smells can make it harder for developers to understand the system, increasing the **cognitive load** when trying to maintain or add new features.
- **Reduced Maintainability**: Smelly code tends to accumulate over time and can become harder to change without introducing bugs.
- **Scalability Issues**: Code smells often indicate that a system is poorly designed, and the issues can hinder the system's ability to scale properly.

Recognizing and addressing code smells is a key part of writing clean, maintainable code.

Common Code Smells and How to Recognize Them

1. Long Methods

A **long method** is a method that tries to accomplish too much, which makes it difficult to follow and understand. These methods often do several unrelated things, violating the **Single Responsibility Principle** (SRP). The longer the method, the harder it is to maintain, test, or debug.

How to Recognize It:

- Methods that are several dozen lines long.
- Methods that include too many loops, conditionals, or nested blocks.
- Methods that handle multiple concerns, such as data processing, UI updates, and database access all in one.

Example: Long Method

cpp

```cpp
void processOrder(Order order) {
    validateOrder(order);
    checkInventory(order);
    calculateTax(order);
    applyDiscount(order);
    updateDatabase(order);
    sendConfirmationEmail(order);
    printReceipt(order);
}
```

This method handles multiple responsibilities—validating, calculating, updating, and sending emails. It's a **smelly** method because it does too much.

111

Refactor:

Split the method into smaller, more focused methods, each handling one responsibility.

cpp

```cpp
void processOrder(Order order) {
    validateOrder(order);
    updateOrderDetails(order);
    sendOrderConfirmation(order);
}

void validateOrder(Order order) {
    // Validation logic
}

void updateOrderDetails(Order order) {
    // Inventory check, tax calculation,
    discount, and database update
}

void sendOrderConfirmation(Order order) {
    // Send email and print receipt
}
```

By refactoring, each method now has **one responsibility**, making the code easier to read and maintain.

2. Large Classes

A **large class** has too many responsibilities and often violates the **Single Responsibility Principle (SRP)**. Large classes become difficult to maintain, as they tend to have too many methods and variables, often involving multiple concerns that could be better separated.

How to Recognize It:

- Classes that contain too many methods (50+ lines).
- Classes that seem to handle multiple, unrelated tasks.
- A class that becomes a "God class"—centralizing functionality from multiple areas.

Example: Large Class

cpp

```cpp
class OrderManager {
public:
    void createOrder(Order order);
    void validateOrder(Order order);
    void calculateTotal(Order order);
    void updateInventory(Order order);
    void sendInvoice(Order order);
    void handlePayment(Order order);
    void applyDiscount(Order order);
    void generateReport();
};
```

This `OrderManager` class is **doing too much**—it manages orders, handles payments, applies discounts, and generates reports. This violates SRP.

Refactor:

Break the class into smaller, focused classes based on their responsibilities.

cpp

```cpp
class OrderValidator {
public:
    void validateOrder(Order order);
};

class OrderCalculator {
public:
    double calculateTotal(Order order);
};

class PaymentProcessor {
public:
    void handlePayment(Order order);
};

class DiscountManager {
public:
    void applyDiscount(Order order);
```

114

```cpp
};

class ReportGenerator {
public:
    void generateReport();
};
```

By splitting the responsibilities across smaller classes, we adhere to SRP and improve the **maintainability** of the code.

3. Duplicated Code

Duplicate code appears when the same logic is repeated in multiple places in the codebase. This makes maintenance harder because when you need to change the behavior, you must update each occurrence, which increases the risk of errors.

How to Recognize It:

- Identical or near-identical code blocks appearing in different parts of the program.
- Code that performs the same task in multiple methods or classes.

Example: Duplicated Code

cpp

```cpp
double calculateTotalPrice(Order order) {
    double total = order.getPrice();
```

```
    total += order.getTax();
    total -= order.getDiscount();
    return total;
}


double calculateFinalPrice(Order order) {
    double total = order.getPrice();
    total += order.getTax();
    total -= order.getDiscount();
    total += order.getShipping();
    return total;
}
```

The logic for calculating prices is duplicated between
calculateTotalPrice and calculateFinalPrice.

Refactor:

Extract the common logic into a separate method to avoid
duplication.

cpp

```
double calculateBasePrice(Order order) {
    double total = order.getPrice();
    total += order.getTax();
    total -= order.getDiscount();
    return total;
}
```

```
double calculateTotalPrice(Order order) {
    return calculateBasePrice(order);
}

double calculateFinalPrice(Order order) {
    double total = calculateBasePrice(order);
    total += order.getShipping();
    return total;
}
```

Now, the logic for calculating the base price is shared between both methods, reducing duplication.

4. God Objects and Tight Coupling

A **God Object** is an object that knows too much or does too many things. It typically has high **coupling** with other objects and a large number of responsibilities. Tight coupling refers to situations where classes or modules depend heavily on one another, making it difficult to change one part of the system without affecting the others.

How to Recognize It:

- A single class that controls a large number of interactions or processes.
- A class that has too many dependencies or interacts with many other classes in complex ways.

117

Example: God Object

cpp

```
class OrderManager {
public:
    void processOrder(Order order) {
        orderValidator.validate(order);
        paymentProcessor.processPayment(order);

inventoryManager.updateInventory(order);
        shippingService.prepareShipping(order);
    }
};
```

In this example, `OrderManager` acts as a **God Object**, controlling the entire order process and interacting with many other classes.

Refactor:

Break down responsibilities and delegate tasks to more specialized classes to reduce coupling.

cpp

```
class OrderProcessor {
public:
    void validateOrder(Order order);
    void processPayment(Order order);
```

```
    void updateInventory(Order order);
    void prepareShipping(Order order);
};

class OrderManager {
private:
    OrderProcessor orderProcessor;
public:
    void processOrder(Order order) {
        orderProcessor.validateOrder(order);
        orderProcessor.processPayment(order);
        orderProcessor.updateInventory(order);
        orderProcessor.prepareShipping(order);
    }
};
```

By refactoring, we reduce the coupling between the OrderManager and other services, and make the OrderProcessor more cohesive.

5. Overuse of Conditionals and Flags

Using **too many conditionals** or **flags** in your code can be a code smell. They often indicate that the code is trying to handle multiple behaviors within one function, which can lead to messy and unmanageable code.

119

- Functions or methods that have many `if`, `else`, or `switch` statements, often for handling different types of behavior.
- Flags that alter the behavior of methods in various ways.

Example: Overuse of Conditionals

cpp

```cpp
void generateReport(int reportType) {
    if (reportType == 1) {
        // Generate sales report
    } else if (reportType == 2) {
        // Generate inventory report
    } else if (reportType == 3) {
        // Generate user activity report
    }
}
```

This method is becoming difficult to extend. Adding a new report type requires modifying the method.

Refactor:

Use **polymorphism** or **strategy patterns** to eliminate the need for conditionals.

cpp

```cpp
class Report {
public:
    virtual void generate() = 0;
};

class SalesReport : public Report {
public:
    void generate() override {
        // Sales report logic
    }
};

class InventoryReport : public Report {
public:
    void generate() override {
        // Inventory report logic
    }
};

class ReportManager {
public:
    void generateReport(Report& report) {
        report.generate();
    }
};
```

By using polymorphism, each report type is a class with its own behavior, eliminating the need for conditionals and improving code maintainability.

Techniques to Refactor Code Smells into Clean Code

1. Extract Methods

For long methods, break them down into smaller methods, each handling a single responsibility.

2. Use Design Patterns

For common issues such as excessive conditionals or redundant code, consider using **design patterns** like the **Strategy Pattern**, **Factory Pattern**, or **Observer Pattern** to decouple code and make it more modular.

3. Apply SOLID Principles

The SOLID principles can help resolve many code smells by ensuring that each class has a **single responsibility**, is **open for extension**, and **closed for modification**.

4. Simplify Conditionals

Refactor complex conditionals by breaking them into smaller, more understandable pieces. Use **polymorphism** to handle different behaviors, or leverage the **Strategy Pattern** for more flexible decision-making.

Conclusion

Code smells are common signs that indicate your code may need refactoring. By recognizing and addressing smells such as **long methods, large classes, duplicated code, God objects**, and **overuse of conditionals**, you can significantly improve the readability, maintainability, and scalability of your code. The techniques discussed in this chapter, such as **method extraction, design patterns**, and applying the **SOLID principles**, can help you transform smelly code into clean, efficient, and modular code. By continuously addressing code smells, you can ensure that your software remains **flexible, maintainable**, and **scalable** over time.

CHAPTER 9

REFACTORING TECHNIQUES: IMPROVING LEGACY CODE

Refactoring is a vital process in software development, especially when working with legacy code. It allows developers to improve the **structure**, **readability**, and **maintainability** of existing code without altering its functionality. In this chapter, we will explore why **refactoring** is necessary, how to refactor code without changing its behavior, when and how to refactor, and provide a **step-by-step refactoring process**. Additionally, we will review **case studies** of refactoring in real-world applications to understand how these techniques are applied in practice.

Why Refactoring is Necessary for Maintaining Clean Code

Over time, as software evolves, it becomes more complex and harder to maintain. Legacy code often accumulates **technical debt**, which can slow down development and increase the risk of bugs. **Refactoring** helps eliminate this debt by restructuring the code to make it **cleaner, more efficient**, and **easier to modify** without changing its functionality.

Benefits of Refactoring:

- **Improved Readability**: Clear, well-structured code is easier for new developers to understand and work with.
- **Better Maintainability**: Refactoring reduces the chances of introducing errors when adding new features or fixing bugs.
- **Enhanced Performance**: Refactoring can optimize code, making it run more efficiently.
- **Increased Flexibility**: Clean code is easier to extend and adapt to new requirements.
- **Reduced Technical Debt**: By improving the structure, you make future changes easier and less costly.

Refactoring Without Changing Functionality

A key principle of refactoring is to **preserve the existing functionality** of the software. Refactoring involves making changes to the **internal structure** of the code—such as renaming variables, splitting large functions, or extracting classes—without altering the **observable behavior** of the system.

How to Refactor Without Changing Functionality:

- **Write Tests Before Refactoring**: Ensure that there are existing unit tests or write new ones to verify the code's correctness before making changes.

- **Refactor in Small Steps**: Make incremental changes and frequently run tests to ensure that functionality is preserved.

- **Avoid Making Behavioral Changes**: Focus on improving readability, reducing duplication, or simplifying logic, rather than modifying how the software behaves.

Example: Refactoring Without Changing Behavior

cpp

```cpp
// Before refactoring: Long function with multiple responsibilities
double calculateDiscountedPrice(double price, double discount) {
    double discountAmount = price * discount;
    double discountedPrice = price - discountAmount;
    if (discountedPrice < 0) {
        discountedPrice = 0;  // Ensure price is not negative
    }
    return discountedPrice;
```

```
}

// After refactoring: Breaking down into smaller
functions
double   calculateDiscountAmount(double   price,
double discount) {
    return price * discount;
}

double ensureNonNegativePrice(double price) {
    if (price < 0) {
        return 0;
    }
    return price;
}

double   calculateDiscountedPrice(double   price,
double discount) {
    double           discountAmount           =
calculateDiscountAmount(price, discount);
    double   discountedPrice   =   price   -
discountAmount;
    return
ensureNonNegativePrice(discountedPrice);
}
```

In this example, the code was refactored into smaller methods (`calculateDiscountAmount` and `ensureNonNegativePrice`) without changing the original logic. **Tests** would ensure that the **behavior** remains the same while the **structure** improves.

When and How to Refactor Code

Refactoring should be done at the right time to avoid disrupting development and introducing unnecessary complexity. Here are some indicators that suggest when to refactor and guidelines for doing it effectively.

When to Refactor Code:

1. **When the Codebase Becomes Hard to Maintain**: If adding new features or fixing bugs becomes harder due to tangled or complex code, it's time to refactor.
2. **When You Notice Code Smells**: If you spot common **code smells** (like long methods, large classes, duplicated code), it's a good time to consider refactoring.
3. **When Adding New Features**: If you need to add new features but find that the existing code is hard to extend or adapt, it's often a good idea to refactor to accommodate these changes.
4. **When Preparing for Future Changes**: If you foresee upcoming changes or scaling needs, refactoring can help ensure the code is flexible and ready for modifications.

128

How to Refactor Code:

1. **Start with Tests**: Ensure that the current functionality is well-tested, and write additional tests if necessary. This will serve as a safety net during refactoring.

2. **Make Small, Incremental Changes**: Rather than a massive overhaul, refactor small parts of the codebase incrementally. This reduces the risk of introducing new issues.

3. **Refactor One Problem at a Time**: Focus on solving one issue or improving one part of the code at a time (e.g., extracting a method or reducing duplication).

4. **Use Version Control**: Commit changes to version control (e.g., Git) frequently to track progress and make it easier to roll back changes if needed.

5. **Test Continuously**: After each small refactor, run tests to ensure that functionality has been preserved.

The Refactoring Process Step-by-Step

Refactoring is a process that can be broken down into manageable steps. Here's a step-by-step guide to refactoring code efficiently:

Step 1: Understand the Current Code

Before making any changes, thoroughly understand the code you plan to refactor. Look at the flow of the logic, the relationships between classes and functions, and identify any **pain points** or areas that could be improved.

Step 2: Write Unit Tests

Ensure that the code is properly **tested** before refactoring. If necessary, write unit tests that cover the current behavior of the system. These tests will serve as a **baseline** to ensure that nothing breaks during the refactor.

Step 3: Identify Areas for Refactoring

Look for **code smells** such as long methods, duplicate code, or overly complex logic. Focus on areas that are **difficult to maintain** or **prone to errors**. Start by prioritizing areas that are **most important** or **likely to change** in the future.

Step 4: Refactor Incrementally

Start making changes to improve the code's structure. Refactor in small, manageable steps. For example:

- **Extract methods** to break down large functions.
- **Rename variables and functions** to clarify their purpose.

- **Simplify logic** by removing unnecessary complexity.

Step 5: Run Tests After Each Change

After making a small change, immediately run your tests to ensure that you haven't unintentionally broken anything. If the tests pass, you can safely proceed with the next step.

Step 6: Repeat Until Refactored

Continue the process of incremental refactoring until the code has been fully refactored to improve readability, reduce duplication, and simplify logic. At each step, make sure that functionality is preserved, and tests pass.

Step 7: Review and Refactor Again (if necessary)

Once you've completed the first round of refactoring, take a step back and review the code. If any further improvements can be made, continue to refine the code until it is clean, simple, and maintainable.

Case Studies of Refactoring in Real-World Applications

1. Refactoring a Legacy E-commerce System

An e-commerce platform had a monolithic codebase where various features like **order processing**, **inventory management**, and **payment processing** were tightly coupled in a single class. This made it difficult to maintain and extend the application.

Refactoring Process:

- **Identify Areas of Concern**: The `OrderManager` class was responsible for multiple tasks, making it difficult to add new payment methods or integrate with different inventory systems.
- **Incremental Refactoring**: The `OrderManager` class was broken down into smaller classes with distinct responsibilities: `OrderProcessor`, `PaymentHandler`, and `InventoryManager`.
- **Test-Driven Refactoring**: After each change, unit tests were run to ensure that the functionality of the system remained intact.

2. Refactoring a Legacy Banking System

A legacy banking system contained complex methods for handling transactions, which included multiple responsibilities such as **account validation**, **fund transfer**, and **transaction**

logging. This made it challenging to track errors or add new transaction features.

Refactoring Process:

- **Separate Concerns**: The code was refactored to separate each responsibility into its own class. For example, `AccountValidator`, `FundTransfer`, and `TransactionLogger` were created as separate classes.
- **Simplify Logic**: Complex methods were broken down into smaller, more manageable functions, making the code more readable and maintainable.
- **Test Coverage**: Unit tests were written for each class to ensure functionality was preserved after refactoring.

Conclusion

Refactoring is an essential part of the software development lifecycle. It allows developers to **improve** the structure of legacy code while ensuring that its functionality remains intact. By recognizing code smells and applying systematic refactoring techniques, you can make your codebase more **maintainable**, **scalable**, and **flexible**. The **step-by-step process** outlined in this chapter—starting from understanding the code, writing tests, identifying problem areas, and making incremental changes—ensures that refactoring can be done safely and effectively.

In real-world applications, refactoring is often an ongoing process that helps maintain code quality over time. By applying refactoring techniques to your legacy systems, you'll ensure that they remain adaptable and ready for future changes, while reducing the risk of introducing new bugs.

CHAPTER 10

TEST-DRIVEN DEVELOPMENT (TDD): ENSURING CLEAN CODE THROUGH TESTING

Test-Driven Development (TDD) is a software development practice that focuses on writing tests **before** writing the code that makes the tests pass. By following the TDD process, developers can ensure that their code is well-tested from the start, leading to better architecture, fewer bugs, and cleaner, more maintainable code. This chapter will explore the fundamentals of TDD, discuss why writing tests before code leads to better design, and demonstrate the value of unit tests and automated testing in ensuring clean code. We will also look at how TDD influences code design and review real-world examples of how TDD has positively impacted maintainability.

Introduction to TDD

Test-Driven Development is a development approach where you write tests before writing the corresponding production code. It follows a strict cycle of **Red-Green-Refactor**:

1. **Red**: Write a failing test that defines the desired functionality.
2. **Green**: Write the minimal amount of code necessary to pass the test.
3. **Refactor**: Improve the code while ensuring the test still passes.

TDD emphasizes writing **small, incremental tests** for each feature, ensuring that new code doesn't introduce bugs and that the software is always in a **working state**. This approach leads to cleaner, more maintainable code because the development process is guided by the tests that define the expected behavior of the system.

Benefits of TDD:

- **Early Bug Detection**: TDD ensures that issues are caught early in the development cycle, reducing the likelihood of defects in production.
- **Cleaner Code**: The focus on passing small tests encourages developers to write simpler, well-structured code that meets specific, well-defined requirements.
- **Improved Documentation**: Tests serve as documentation, clearly describing the intended behavior of the system.

- **Confidence in Refactoring**: Since tests are written first, developers can confidently refactor the code, knowing that any breakage will be caught by failing tests.

Writing Tests Before Code for Cleaner Architecture

Writing tests before the code itself is the cornerstone of **Test-Driven Development (TDD)**. This may seem counterintuitive to some, but it actually leads to **better-designed systems**. By starting with tests, you ensure that the code you write has a clear purpose and meets a specific requirement.

1. Forces Developers to Think in Terms of Behavior

When you write tests first, you define the behavior of the system **before** you implement it. This leads to **better-designed code** since you're thinking about how the system should behave rather than focusing on how to implement the solution. The tests act as a blueprint, guiding the development process.

2. Helps with Designing for Testability

TDD encourages writing **modular, loosely-coupled** code that is easy to test. This results in **cleaner architecture** because you naturally avoid writing monolithic code that is difficult to test and maintain.

Example: Writing Tests First

cpp

```cpp
// Step 1: Write a test (Red)
void testAddition() {
    Calculator calc;
    int result = calc.add(1, 2);
    assert(result == 3);
}

// Step 2: Write minimal code to pass the test
(Green)
class Calculator {
public:
    int add(int a, int b) {
        return a + b;
    }
};
```

In this example, the test is written **before** the add function, ensuring that the function's purpose is clearly defined. The test drives the design of the Calculator class, ensuring that it only contains the necessary logic for addition.

The Importance of Unit Tests and Automated Testing

Unit tests are small, automated tests that focus on testing a **single unit** of functionality, such as a function or method. Unit tests ensure that individual components of the application behave as expected in isolation, without dependencies on other components.

1. Benefits of Unit Testing:

- **Early Detection of Bugs**: Unit tests allow developers to detect issues in their code early in the development process, preventing problems from propagating into later stages.
- **Confidence in Changes**: Having a suite of unit tests enables developers to confidently make changes to the codebase, knowing that any issues will be immediately flagged.
- **Simplifies Debugging**: When a unit test fails, it helps pinpoint the source of the problem quickly, making debugging easier and faster.

2. Benefits of Automated Testing:

- **Efficiency**: Automated tests can be run frequently and consistently, providing immediate feedback on the status of the code.

139

- **Regression Prevention**: Automated tests can be run as part of a **continuous integration pipeline**, ensuring that new code changes do not break existing functionality (i.e., preventing regressions).

- **Cost-Effective**: Automated tests save time and effort in the long run by reducing the need for manual testing, making it easier to test every corner of your codebase regularly.

Example: Writing Unit Tests

cpp

```cpp
// Test the add function
void testAddition() {
    Calculator calc;
    assert(calc.add(2, 3) == 5);
}


// Test the subtract function
void testSubtraction() {
    Calculator calc;
    assert(calc.subtract(5, 3) == 2);
}
```

In this example, the testAddition and testSubtraction functions are automated tests that validate the behavior of the Calculator class. They ensure that both the add and subtract functions perform as expected, improving the **reliability** of the code.

How TDD Influences Code Design

Test-Driven Development has a **profound influence** on how code is structured. It encourages writing small, **modular** pieces of code that can be easily tested, which leads to **cleaner code** overall. Here's how TDD influences design:

1. Forces Simpler Code

TDD encourages writing just enough code to make a test pass, which often results in **simpler** and **more focused** solutions. This is because developers aren't tempted to over-engineer or add unnecessary functionality upfront.

2. Promotes Code Reusability

Because TDD focuses on small, testable units, it often leads to code that is **reusable**. Developers create small, focused methods or classes that can be easily repurposed in different contexts, reducing duplication and increasing efficiency.

3. Reduces the Need for Extensive Refactoring

With tests in place, the code is already structured to be **testable**, meaning refactoring and improving the design later on becomes much easier. TDD promotes writing code that is **modular** and **flexible**, making it easier to adapt and refactor as the project evolves.

4. Ensures Consistent Behavior

By writing tests first, TDD ensures that the **behavior** of the system is defined and consistent. It helps prevent **unexpected side effects** by making sure every change is validated against pre-written tests.

Real-World Examples of TDD and Its Impact on Maintainability

1. Example: Refactoring a Legacy Banking System

A legacy banking system had a huge codebase that was difficult to maintain and extend. Developers often had to manually test each feature after making changes, which led to frequent regressions and **bugs**.

TDD Implementation:

- **Step 1**: Write tests for existing functionality to ensure it's preserved.
- **Step 2**: Refactor the code in small, incremental steps while constantly running tests.
- **Result**: After applying TDD, developers were able to **safely refactor** and **add features** without breaking the system. The **test coverage** ensured that any changes didn't introduce new bugs, making the system easier to maintain.

2. Example: Building an E-commerce Checkout System

An e-commerce company wanted to implement a new **checkout process** that included features like **discount codes, tax calculations**, and **shipping options**.

TDD Implementation:

- **Step 1**: The team wrote unit tests for each feature of the checkout process before writing any code.
- **Step 2**: The code was written in small increments, with tests being run continuously to ensure the new functionality didn't break existing behavior.
- **Result**: TDD ensured that the checkout system was **modular, maintainable**, and **robust**. New features were

added quickly without compromising on quality, and the code was easier to understand and extend in the future.

Conclusion

Test-Driven Development (TDD) is a powerful technique for writing **clean, maintainable, and scalable** code. By writing tests **before** you write code, TDD encourages you to think about the desired behavior and structure of your system upfront, leading to simpler and more modular design. The process of writing **unit tests** and leveraging **automated testing** improves code reliability and reduces the risk of introducing bugs. Additionally, TDD influences code design by promoting **modularity**, **simplicity**, and **flexibility**, resulting in cleaner codebases that are easier to maintain over time.

By implementing TDD in real-world projects, you can **refactor legacy code**, **prevent regressions**, and **ensure clean architecture**. Whether you are starting a new project or working with an existing one, TDD is a valuable practice that leads to better software quality and more confident development.

144

CHAPTER 11

THE ROLE OF UNIT TESTS IN MAINTAINING CLEAN CODE

Unit tests are essential for ensuring the quality, **reliability**, and **maintainability** of software. They serve as a **safety net** for developers, catching bugs early and ensuring that individual components of the system behave as expected. In this chapter, we will explore what makes a good unit test, the differences between **test-first** and **test-last** development, how to structure unit tests for **clarity and readability**, and how to write **maintainable** and **scalable** test cases. Additionally, we will discuss **real-world case studies** of well-tested code in production systems and how unit tests contribute to maintaining clean code.

What Makes a Good Unit Test?

A **good unit test** is one that is **simple, reliable**, and **easy to understand**. It ensures that the unit of code it tests behaves as expected, and it should have several key characteristics:

1. Clear Purpose

Each unit test should focus on **one specific behavior** or requirement of the code. A unit test should be easy to understand, with a clear description of what it is testing.

2. Isolated

A good unit test is **isolated** from other tests, meaning it doesn't depend on external systems, such as databases or third-party services. This isolation ensures that tests can run quickly and independently of external conditions.

3. Fast

Unit tests should be fast to execute, providing immediate feedback on the correctness of the code. If a test takes too long, it can slow down the development cycle and discourage frequent testing.

4. Consistent

A unit test should always produce the same result, given the same inputs. It should not be **flaky**—a good test should pass or fail consistently, providing reliable feedback.

5. Descriptive Assertions

The assertions in unit tests should clearly express the **expected behavior**. Instead of just checking for equality, they should express the expected outcome in a way that is easy to understand.

Example of a Good Unit Test

cpp

```
// Testing the addition of two numbers
void testAddition() {
    Calculator calc;
    int result = calc.add(2, 3);
    assert(result == 5);    // Descriptive
assertion of expected outcome
}
```

In this example, the test clearly indicates that it is testing the **addition** functionality of the `Calculator` class, and the assertion ensures that the result is equal to 5, which is the expected outcome.

Test-First vs. Test-Last Development

There are two main approaches to writing unit tests: **test-first** and **test-last** development. Both have their pros and cons, but understanding the differences between the two approaches can help you choose the best method for your development process.

1. Test-First Development (TDD)

Test-first development, often associated with **Test-Driven Development (TDD)**, involves writing **tests before writing the actual code**. The process follows a strict **Red-Green-Refactor** cycle:

- **Red**: Write a test that fails (since the functionality is not implemented yet).
- **Green**: Write just enough code to pass the test.
- **Refactor**: Clean up the code while ensuring that the test still passes.

Benefits of Test-First Development:

- **Design Focused**: Writing tests first forces developers to think about the design and requirements upfront, leading to better-organized code.
- **Small Increments**: TDD encourages small, incremental changes, reducing the chances of introducing large, complex bugs.
- **Better Test Coverage**: Writing tests before the code ensures that all aspects of the code are covered by tests.

Example:

cpp

```
// Step 1: Write the test (Red)
```

```
void testAddition() {
    Calculator calc;
    assert(calc.add(2, 3) == 5);
}


// Step 2: Write minimal code to make the test
pass (Green)
class Calculator {
public:
    int add(int a, int b) {
        return a + b;
    }
};
```

2. Test-Last Development

Test-last development involves writing the code first and then writing tests afterward. In this approach, developers typically write code to fulfill a specific requirement and then create tests to validate that the code meets the requirement.

Benefits of Test-Last Development:

- **Faster to Start**: Developers can begin coding immediately without having to write tests first.
- **Flexibility**: Test-last development allows developers to write the code the way they think is best without worrying about writing tests upfront.

Drawbacks:

- **Incomplete Test Coverage**: Tests are often added after the code is written, meaning some aspects of the code may not be covered by tests.
- **Potential for Bad Design**: Without the guidance of tests, developers may design the code poorly, resulting in a less modular and harder-to-maintain system.

Example:

cpp

```cpp
// Step 1: Write the code (without tests)
class Calculator {
public:
    int add(int a, int b) {
        return a + b;
    }
};

// Step 2: Write tests afterward
void testAddition() {
    Calculator calc;
    assert(calc.add(2, 3) == 5);
}
```

Structuring Unit Tests for Clarity and Readability

Unit tests should be **easy to read** and understand, just like the production code they are testing. Clear and well-structured tests improve **maintainability** and **collaboration**, especially when working with a team.

1. Organize Tests by Functionality

Tests should be grouped based on the functionality they test. This makes it easier to locate specific tests and maintain them as the code evolves.

Example: Organizing Tests

cpp

```cpp
// Group tests related to addition functionality
void testAdditionWithPositiveNumbers() {
    Calculator calc;
    assert(calc.add(2, 3) == 5);
}

void testAdditionWithNegativeNumbers() {
    Calculator calc;
    assert(calc.add(-2, -3) == -5);
}

// Group tests related to subtraction
functionality
void testSubtractionWithPositiveNumbers() {
    Calculator calc;
```

```cpp
    assert(calc.subtract(5, 3) == 2);
}
```

2. Use Descriptive Test Names

Each test method should have a descriptive name that clearly explains what the test is checking. This will make the test suite more understandable and easier to maintain.

Example:

cpp

```cpp
// Descriptive test name
void
testAddition_WithPositiveNumbers_ReturnsCorrect
Result() {
    Calculator calc;
    assert(calc.add(2, 3) == 5);
}
```

3. Keep Tests Small and Focused

Each unit test should focus on a **single behavior** or unit of code. Keeping tests small and focused ensures that they are easy to understand and maintain.

Example:

cpp

```cpp
// Bad: Multiple assertions in a single test
void testOrderProcessing() {
```

```
    Order order;
    assert(order.addItem("Item 1"));
    assert(order.calculateTotal() == 100);
    assert(order.applyDiscount() == 90);
}


// Good: Separate tests for each behavior
void testAddItem() {
    Order order;
    assert(order.addItem("Item 1"));
}


void testCalculateTotal() {
    Order order;
    assert(order.calculateTotal() == 100);
}


void testApplyDiscount() {
    Order order;
    assert(order.applyDiscount() == 90);
}
```

Writing Maintainable and Scalable Test Cases

For unit tests to be effective in the long run, they must be **maintainable** and **scalable**. As your codebase grows, so too will the number of tests. Therefore, it's important to follow best practices for writing tests that are easy to maintain and extend.

1. Avoid Hardcoding Test Data

Whenever possible, use variables or constants instead of hardcoding data into the tests. This makes tests easier to change and extend in the future.

Example:

cpp

```cpp
// Bad: Hardcoded data in tests
void testAddition() {
    assert(add(2, 3) == 5);
}

// Good: Using variables or constants
const int NUM1 = 2;
const int NUM2 = 3;

void testAddition() {
    assert(add(NUM1, NUM2) == 5);
}
```

2. Isolate Tests from External Dependencies

Tests should be isolated from external systems such as databases or APIs. You can use **mock objects** or **stubs** to simulate external systems and ensure that tests are independent of outside factors.

Example: Using Mock Objects

cpp

```
class Database {
public:
    virtual void saveData(const std::string&
data) = 0;
};


class MockDatabase : public Database {
public:
    void saveData(const std::string& data)
override {
        // Simulate saving data
    }
};


// Test using the mock object
void testSaveData() {
    MockDatabase mockDB;
    mockDB.saveData("test data");
    assert(mockDB.isDataSaved());  // Check if
data was "saved" correctly
}
```

3. Use Assertions Wisely

Unit tests typically use assertions to check the expected output. However, it's important to use assertions that clearly communicate the expected outcome of the test.

Example:

cpp

```
// Bad: Unclear assertion message
assert(result == 100);

// Good: Descriptive assertion message
assert(result == expectedValue, "Expected result
to be 100, but got " + std::to_string(result));
```

Case Studies of Well-Tested Code in Production Systems

1. Case Study: E-Commerce Checkout System

In an **e-commerce checkout system**, the development team adopted TDD to ensure that all key operations—such as **order validation**, **payment processing**, and **shipping calculation**—were properly tested. Each feature was accompanied by comprehensive unit tests, ensuring that **refactoring** or adding new functionality wouldn't break the existing system.

Outcome:

- Reduced **bugs** during development.
- Enabled **faster iterations** of new features without fear of regressions.

- Improved **confidence** in the reliability of the checkout system.

2. Case Study: Financial Trading Platform

A **financial trading platform** relied heavily on unit tests to validate complex algorithms for calculating trades, managing portfolios, and handling market data. The development team wrote tests for each algorithmic function before writing the implementation.

Outcome:

- Provided a **robust safety net**, preventing errors in trading logic.
- Allowed for **frequent updates** to trading algorithms without breaking core features.
- Ensured high **accuracy** and **reliability**, which are critical in the financial domain.

Conclusion

Unit tests play a crucial role in maintaining **clean, reliable, and maintainable code**. They provide a safety net that ensures individual units of code behave as expected and that changes to the system do not introduce new bugs. By adopting **test-first**

development and following best practices for writing maintainable tests, developers can ensure that their codebase remains easy to manage as it grows. Case studies demonstrate how **well-tested systems** contribute to long-term **scalability** and **reliability**, making unit testing an indispensable part of any software development process.

CHAPTER 12

AVOIDING DUPLICATION: DRY AND KISS PRINCIPLES

In the world of software development, two key principles—**Don't Repeat Yourself (DRY)** and **Keep It Simple, Stupid (KISS)**—are foundational to creating clean, maintainable, and efficient code. These principles emphasize the importance of **eliminating redundancy**, **simplifying designs**, and **maximizing code reusability**. In this chapter, we will explore the **DRY** and **KISS** principles, their importance, and how they can help you avoid code duplication, improve reusability, and write more concise code. Additionally, we will look at **real-world examples** of applying these principles to large codebases.

The Don't Repeat Yourself (DRY) Principle

The **DRY** principle, introduced by **Andy Hunt** and **Dave Thomas** in their book *The Pragmatic Programmer*, states that **every piece of knowledge** in your system should be represented in **one place** only. This principle helps avoid duplication in the codebase, which leads to more maintainable and less error-prone code.

Why DRY Matters:

1. **Reduces Redundancy**: Duplication of code leads to unnecessary redundancy. If the same logic appears in multiple places, any change to that logic must be made in every location where it's used. This can be error-prone and time-consuming.

2. **Improves Maintainability**: By consolidating logic into a single location, changes can be made more easily, ensuring consistency throughout the codebase.

3. **Prevents Bugs**: When logic is duplicated, it increases the chance of bugs because changes made in one place might not be reflected in others.

Examples of Violating DRY:

cpp

```cpp
// Bad: Duplicate logic in multiple places
double calculateDiscount(double price, double discount) {
    return price * discount;
}

double calculateFinalPrice(double price, double discount, double tax) {
    double discountedPrice = price * discount;
    double finalPrice = discountedPrice + (discountedPrice * tax);
```

```
    return finalPrice;
}
```

In this example, the logic for calculating the discounted price (`price * discount`) is duplicated. If we want to modify this logic, we would need to update it in two places, risking inconsistency.

Refactor to Adhere to DRY:

cpp

```
// Good: Centralized logic for calculating discounts
double calculateDiscount(double price, double discount) {
    return price * discount;
}

double calculateFinalPrice(double price, double discount, double tax) {
    double discountedPrice = calculateDiscount(price, discount);
    double finalPrice = discountedPrice + (discountedPrice * tax);
    return finalPrice;
}
```

In this refactor, the `calculateDiscount` function centralizes the logic for applying a discount, adhering to the DRY principle.

Now, if we need to change how the discount is calculated, we only need to update the `calculateDiscount` function.

The Keep It Simple, Stupid (KISS) Principle

The **KISS** principle is one of the simplest yet most powerful design philosophies. It suggests that software should be **as simple as possible** and avoid unnecessary complexity. The key idea is that **complexity leads to bugs, makes code harder to maintain**, and reduces clarity. **Simple solutions are easier to understand, test, and modify**.

Why KISS Matters:

1. **Reduces Complexity**: Simple solutions are more straightforward, making it easier to **read, understand**, and **maintain** the code.

2. **Minimizes Bugs**: By avoiding unnecessary complexity, you minimize the chance of introducing defects. Simple code is less prone to errors because it's easier to reason about.

3. **Promotes Flexibility**: Simpler code is easier to extend, as it's easier to understand and modify without introducing unintended side effects.

Examples of Violating KISS:

cpp

```cpp
// Bad: Unnecessary complexity and over-
engineering
class Order {
public:
    double calculateTotalPrice() {
        double discount = 0;
        if (this->items > 5) {
            discount = 0.1;
        } else if (this->items > 10) {
            discount = 0.15;
        }
        return this->basePrice * (1 - discount);
    }
};
```

In this example, the logic for calculating discounts is **over-engineered** with an unnecessary number of conditions that could be simplified.

Refactor to Adhere to KISS:

cpp

```cpp
// Good: Simplified logic using a constant
discount
class Order {
public:
```

```
double calculateTotalPrice() {
    double discount = this->items > 10 ? 0.15
: (this->items > 5 ? 0.1 : 0);
        return this->basePrice * (1 - discount);
    }
};
```

The refactor simplifies the logic, reducing unnecessary complexity while maintaining the same functionality. It applies a **ternary operator** for a more compact, readable approach.

How to Avoid Code Duplication and Improve Reusability

To adhere to the DRY and KISS principles, it's essential to think about code **modularity**, **reusability**, and **simplicity**. Here are a few strategies for avoiding code duplication and improving reusability:

1. Use Functions and Methods Wisely

Encapsulate repetitive logic into **functions** or **methods**. This promotes **reusability** and makes the code more **maintainable**.

```cpp
// Avoid duplication
```

```cpp
double    applyDiscount(double    price,    double
discount) {
    return price * discount;
}


double    calculateTotal(double    price,    double
discount) {
    return applyDiscount(price, discount);
}
```

2. Leverage Inheritance and Polymorphism

In object-oriented design, **inheritance** and **polymorphism** can be used to reuse common functionality and avoid code duplication in subclasses.

cpp

```cpp
// Base class with common functionality
class Shape {
public:
    virtual double area() = 0;
};


// Derived classes with specific implementations
class Rectangle : public Shape {
private:
    double width, height;
public:
    double area() override {
```

165

```
        return width * height;
    }
};


class Circle : public Shape {
private:
    double radius;
public:
    double area() override {
        return 3.14 * radius * radius;
    }
};
```

In this example, both `Rectangle` and `Circle` share the common `area()` method interface, allowing for code reuse and avoiding duplication.

3. Utilize Libraries and Frameworks

Many programming languages have libraries or frameworks that offer **pre-built functionality** that you can use, instead of reinventing the wheel.

- **Example**: Instead of writing your own HTTP request handling, use a library like **libcurl** in C++ or **Requests** in Python.

4. Refactor Large Classes into Smaller, Focused Ones

If a class is too large and has multiple responsibilities, split it into smaller, more cohesive classes. This reduces code duplication and improves the clarity of the code.

Real-World Examples of Applying DRY and KISS to Large Codebases

1. Refactoring a Legacy Financial Application

In a **legacy financial application**, developers found multiple pieces of code for calculating tax rates, applying discounts, and processing transactions scattered throughout the codebase. These repeated logic blocks made the code **hard to maintain** and **error-prone**.

How DRY and KISS Helped:

- **DRY**: By centralizing the calculation logic into reusable functions and services (e.g., `TaxCalculator`, `DiscountApplier`), the developers removed duplication and ensured consistency.
- **KISS**: Complex, nested conditional logic was simplified using **ternary operators** and **helper methods**, reducing

the complexity of calculations and making the code easier to understand.

Outcome:

- Refactoring resulted in more **modular** code, where each component was responsible for only one task. This made the system easier to maintain and extend.

2. Simplifying a Web Application

In a web application for **e-commerce**, the developers initially implemented discount logic that was complex, difficult to extend, and prone to errors. The logic involved multiple nested **if-else** conditions to calculate the final price based on discount rules.

How DRY and KISS Helped:

- **DRY**: The discount logic was **centralized** into a dedicated class, eliminating redundancy across the application.
- **KISS**: The overly complex logic was replaced with simpler, rule-based conditions and **helper methods**, reducing the overall complexity.

Outcome:

- The **codebase** became cleaner and more **maintainable**, and it became easier to **add new types of discounts** without introducing complexity or redundancy.

3. Refactoring a Customer Relationship Management (CRM) System

A CRM system had separate modules for handling customer data, generating reports, and sending communications. However, the code for creating customer records was **duplicated** across several parts of the system, leading to frequent bugs and maintenance issues.

How DRY and KISS Helped:

- **DRY**: The process for creating and updating customer records was **centralized** into a `CustomerService` class, eliminating duplicate logic.
- **KISS**: The system was simplified by reducing the number of complex conditions and nested loops. The code was **restructured** into smaller, more understandable functions.

Outcome:

- The refactoring improved the **reliability** of the CRM system, reducing **bugs** and making the system easier to update and extend.

Conclusion

The **DRY** and **KISS** principles are essential for maintaining clean code. By adhering to DRY, developers can reduce redundancy, improve maintainability, and ensure consistency. KISS encourages simplifying complex code, making it easier to understand and extend. Together, these principles help create **modular**, **reusable**, and **scalable** codebases that are easy to maintain and improve over time.

In real-world applications, applying DRY and KISS principles often leads to **simplified architectures**, **improved performance**, and **reduced bugs**. Whether you're refactoring a legacy system or starting from scratch, these principles provide a solid foundation for writing clean, maintainable code.

CHAPTER 13

HANDLING ERRORS AND EXCEPTIONS IN A CLEAN WAY

Handling errors and exceptions in a **clean and efficient** manner is critical for writing **reliable** and **maintainable** code. Unhandled errors or poorly managed exceptions can lead to **bugs, system crashes**, and a **poor user experience**. In this chapter, we will explore best practices for handling exceptions in a way that keeps your code **readable, robust**, and **scalable**. We'll also dive into how to define **clear error messages, create custom exceptions**, and understand **when to use exceptions** and **when to avoid them**. Finally, we will discuss real-world examples of clean error handling in production systems.

Best Practices for Handling Exceptions in a Clean, Readable Manner

To maintain **clean code**, exceptions should be handled in a way that doesn't clutter the logic or compromise readability. The **exception handling code** should be **simple** and **self-explanatory**, and it should avoid introducing complexity.

171

1. Use Try-Catch Blocks Sparingly

While **try-catch** blocks are essential for handling exceptions, they should not be overused. Wrapping entire blocks of code in `try-catch` should be avoided. Instead, you should only catch exceptions when you **can handle them** meaningfully.

Bad Practice: Overusing `try-catch` Blocks

cpp

```
try {
    // Some logic
    // Some other logic
    someFunctionThatMightThrow();
} catch (std::exception& e) {
    // Catching exception but doing nothing
meaningful with it
}
```

This approach is unhelpful because it catches an exception and doesn't do anything useful with it, like logging or correcting the error. It also hides potential bugs in the code.

Good Practice: Catching Only Specific Exceptions

Instead of a blanket `catch`, you should **catch only the exceptions** you expect and know how to handle.

cpp

```cpp
try {
    someFunctionThatMightThrow();
} catch (const InvalidInputException& e) {
    // Handle invalid input error
    std::cerr << "Invalid input: " << e.what() <<
std::endl;
} catch (const FileReadException& e) {
    // Handle file read error
    std::cerr << "File read error: " << e.what()
<< std::endl;
}
```

This approach ensures that you catch and handle only **specific exceptions**, providing a more **targeted** and **appropriate response**.

2. Avoid Catching Generic Exceptions

Catching generic exceptions, such as `std::exception`, can lead to ambiguity and make the code difficult to debug. It is better to catch more specific exceptions, so you can properly handle different error types.

Bad Practice: Catching a Generic Exception

cpp

```cpp
try {
    someFunctionThatMightThrow();
```

```cpp
} catch (std::exception& e) {
    // Catching a generic exception is too broad
    std::cerr << "An error occurred" << std::endl;
}
```

Good Practice: Catching Specific Exceptions

cpp

```cpp
try {
    someFunctionThatMightThrow();
} catch (const FileNotFoundException& e) {
    std::cerr << "File not found: " << e.what() << std::endl;
} catch (const DatabaseConnectionException& e) {
    std::cerr << "Database connection error: " << e.what() << std::endl;
}
```

This improves clarity by handling different exception types individually and appropriately.

Defining Clear Error Messages and Handling Unexpected States

When an exception occurs, the error message should be **clear**, **informative**, and **easy to understand**. This helps developers quickly understand what went wrong and where the issue lies.

1. Provide Clear, Contextual Information

Always provide **contextual information** in error messages, so it's clear what caused the failure.

Good Practice: Providing Contextual Error Messages

cpp

```cpp
void readFile(const std::string& filename) {
    std::ifstream file(filename);
    if (!file.is_open()) {
        throw FileReadException("Failed to open
file: " + filename);
    }
    // Continue processing the file...
}
```

In this example, the error message clearly indicates which file could not be opened, making it easier to debug.

2. Avoid Generic Error Messages

Generic error messages like "Something went wrong" are not helpful. Always be specific about the error and its cause.

Bad Practice: Using Generic Messages

cpp

```
throw std::runtime_error("An error occurred
while processing the request.");
```

Good Practice: Using Specific Messages

cpp

```
throw DatabaseConnectionException("Unable to
connect to the database: " + dbConnectionString);
```

In this example, the error message indicates exactly where the error occurred (database connection) and provides relevant information (connection string).

Creating Custom Exceptions for Better Clarity

Custom exceptions provide more meaningful error handling in your application, allowing you to differentiate between different types of errors. Instead of relying on generic exception classes, create your own exception classes that extend the `std::exception` class.

1. Define Custom Exception Classes

Custom exceptions allow you to represent specific error scenarios clearly and programmatically. These classes can store additional information (e.g., error codes, filenames) relevant to the exception.

Example of Custom Exception

cpp

```cpp
class FileReadException : public std::exception
{
private:
    std::string message;
public:
    explicit                FileReadException(const
std::string& msg) : message(msg) {}

    const char* what() const noexcept override {
        return message.c_str();
    }
};


class DatabaseConnectionException : public
std::exception {
private:
    std::string message;
public:
```

```cpp
    explicit    DatabaseConnectionException(const
std::string& msg) : message(msg) {}

    const char* what() const noexcept override {
        return message.c_str();
    }
};
```

Now, instead of catching a generic `std::exception`, you can catch specific exceptions like `FileReadException` and `DatabaseConnectionException` and handle them appropriately.

2. Store Additional Information in Custom Exceptions

Custom exceptions can also store additional error data, which can be useful for logging or reporting.

cpp

```cpp
class FileReadException : public std::exception
{
private:
    std::string message;
    std::string filename;
public:
    FileReadException(const  std::string&  msg,
const std::string& file)
        : message(msg), filename(file) {}
```

178

```
const char* what() const noexcept override {
    return message.c_str();
}

const std::string& getFilename() const
noexcept {
    return filename;
}
};
```

In this case, the exception not only provides the error message but also stores the filename that caused the error. This is helpful for debugging.

When to Use Exceptions and When to Avoid Them

Exceptions are a powerful tool for handling error conditions in a controlled way, but they should be used judiciously. Overusing exceptions can lead to performance issues and make the code harder to understand.

When to Use Exceptions:

- **Exceptional, Unrecoverable Conditions**: Use exceptions for scenarios that are **exceptional** and cannot be easily recovered from, such as database connection failures, file I/O errors, or network timeouts.

- **Error Handling Across Multiple Layers**: Exceptions are ideal for situations where you need to propagate an error up the call stack without manually handling each layer.

When to Avoid Exceptions:

- **Normal Control Flow**: Avoid using exceptions for situations that are part of the normal control flow. For example, if a function returns a valid result or error message, there is no need to throw an exception.

- **Performance-Sensitive Code**: In performance-critical sections of code (e.g., tight loops), exceptions can introduce overhead and negatively affect performance.

Example: Avoid using exceptions for normal flow control

cpp

```cpp
// Bad: Using exceptions for normal control flow
void processItems(std::vector<int>& items) {
    for (int item : items) {
        if (item < 0) {
            throw    InvalidItemException("Item
cannot be negative");
        }
        // Process item
```

```
    }
}


// Good: Handle error without exceptions
void processItems(std::vector<int>& items) {
    for (int item : items) {
        if (item < 0) {
            std::cerr << "Invalid item: " << item
<< std::endl;
            continue;
        }
        // Process item
    }
}
```

In this case, using an exception to handle a negative item is unnecessary. It's better to log the error and continue processing the other items.

Real-World Examples of Clean Error Handling in Production Code

1. Web Application - HTTP Request Handling

In a web application, when handling HTTP requests, exceptions are often thrown when there is an issue with processing the request (e.g., bad user input or missing parameters). Proper error handling ensures that the system remains functional and provides useful error messages to users.

Example: Handling HTTP request errors

cpp

```cpp
try {
    handleRequest(request);
} catch (const InvalidInputException& e) {
    std::cerr << "Invalid input error: " <<
e.what() << std::endl;
    sendErrorResponse(400, "Bad Request");
} catch (const DatabaseConnectionException& e) {
    std::cerr << "Database connection failed: "
<< e.what() << std::endl;
    sendErrorResponse(500, "Internal Server
Error");
}
```

Here, specific exceptions are caught and handled appropriately, ensuring the system can respond to errors without crashing.

2. Database-Driven Application - Query Failures

In a database-driven application, query failures can be caused by a variety of issues, including connection failures, timeouts, or invalid SQL queries. Using custom exceptions to handle these errors provides clarity and consistency.

182

Example: Handling database query errors

cpp

```cpp
try {
    executeQuery("SELECT * FROM users");
} catch (const DatabaseQueryException& e) {
    std::cerr << "Query execution failed: " <<
e.what() << std::endl;
    rollbackTransaction();
}
```

This example uses a custom `DatabaseQueryException` to handle any errors specific to database queries, improving the **clarity** and **maintainability** of error handling.

Conclusion

Clean error handling is a fundamental aspect of writing reliable and maintainable code. By following best practices for handling exceptions, defining clear error messages, creating custom exceptions, and knowing when to use or avoid exceptions, you can ensure that your code is robust, easy to debug, and scalable. With real-world examples, we've seen how clean error handling can improve system stability, enhance user experience, and make the codebase easier to maintain over time. Clean error handling is not just about managing failure; it's about building **trust** and **reliability** into your software systems.

CHAPTER 14

PERFORMANCE VS. READABILITY: FINDING THE BALANCE

In software development, there's often a delicate balance between writing **high-performance** code and maintaining **readability**. While performance is crucial, especially in resource-intensive applications, readability ensures that the code is easy to understand, modify, and extend. This chapter explores the tension between performance and readability, providing best practices for when optimization is necessary, how to avoid premature optimization, and how to write code that maintains both high performance and clarity. We will also look at case studies from real-world applications where this balance was achieved.

When Optimization is Necessary: Profiling and Performance Testing

Optimization is necessary when performance bottlenecks in your code affect the overall user experience or system efficiency. However, optimization should not be performed blindly or prematurely. To avoid making unnecessary changes, developers should use **profiling** and **performance testing** to identify areas of code that require optimization.

1. Profiling Code

Profiling is the process of measuring the performance of different parts of a program to identify where most of the computational time is spent. Profiling helps developers focus their efforts on optimizing the most impactful parts of the system, rather than making assumptions or optimizing areas that are not bottlenecks.

Tools for Profiling:

- **gprof**: A profiler for C and C++ that provides information about function call frequencies and execution times.
- **Valgrind**: A tool that can be used to profile programs, detect memory leaks, and analyze performance.
- **Visual Studio Profiler**: A performance profiler for applications written in C++, C#, and other languages.

Example:

bash

```
gprof ./my_program gmon.out > analysis.txt
```

This command generates a performance analysis of your program, allowing you to see which functions consume the most processing time.

2. Performance Testing

Performance testing involves running tests that simulate real-world workloads to see how the system performs under stress. It can reveal **latency issues**, **throughput problems**, and other performance bottlenecks.

Types of Performance Testing:

- **Load Testing**: Determines how the system behaves under heavy traffic.
- **Stress Testing**: Pushes the system beyond its normal operating limits to identify failure points.
- **Benchmarking**: Measures the performance of specific code or features against predefined standards.

When to Optimize?

Optimization should only be performed **after identifying** performance bottlenecks using profiling and testing. Focusing on the **most time-consuming parts of the application** will help achieve the greatest performance gains without overcomplicating the codebase.

Avoiding Premature Optimization

The concept of **premature optimization** was famously described by **Donald Knuth** as the **root of all evil** in programming. Premature optimization occurs when developers attempt to optimize code before they have determined whether optimization is necessary. This often results in **complexity**, **hard-to-read code**, and **wasted effort**.

Why Premature Optimization Is Harmful:

- **Unnecessary Complexity**: Optimization efforts can lead to convoluted code that is harder to read, maintain, and extend.
- **Increased Debugging Difficulty**: Highly optimized code can be harder to debug because it might be less straightforward and more difficult to trace.
- **Wasted Effort**: Optimizing sections of code that don't impact performance may lead to wasted time and resources.

How to Avoid Premature Optimization:

1. **Measure First, Optimize Later**: Before deciding what to optimize, use **profiling** and **performance tests** to identify actual bottlenecks.

2. **Start with Readable Code**: Write code that is **simple** and **readable**. If performance becomes a concern, then focus on optimization only in those critical areas.

3. **Optimize in Small Increments**: Make small optimizations and test their impact on performance. If an optimization doesn't provide a meaningful performance boost, discard it and move on.

Example:

cpp

```
// Bad: Premature optimization
for (int i = 0; i < 1000000; ++i) {
    result += someComplexCalculation(i);
    if (i % 2 == 0) {
        result *= 2;
    }
}


// Good: Simple, readable code first, optimize
later
for (int i = 0; i < 1000000; ++i) {
    result += someComplexCalculation(i);
    if (i % 2 == 0) {
        result *= 2;
    }
}
```

In the first example, the code is overly complex because the developer has prematurely optimized. The second example, which focuses on simplicity, is much more readable. Optimization, if needed, should only be applied after profiling shows that this part of the code is indeed a bottleneck.

Writing Code for Performance Without Sacrificing Readability

Striking the right balance between performance and readability is an art. Writing code that is both performant and easy to understand requires careful consideration of both factors during development.

1. Avoid Over-Optimization

Optimization often involves trade-offs. For instance, using more memory might improve speed, but it could also increase the complexity of your system. Focus on optimizing the areas that will have the **biggest impact** on performance without introducing excessive complexity.

2. Favor Simpler Algorithms

In many cases, an algorithm with **lower time complexity** is the key to achieving better performance, without needing to sacrifice readability. A **simple, O(n)** algorithm might be preferable to a complex **O(n log n)** algorithm if the simpler solution meets performance requirements.

Example: Choosing Simple Over Complex

cpp

```cpp
// Bad: Complex algorithm with unnecessary
overhead
void complexSort(std::vector<int>& data) {
    std::sort(data.begin(), data.end());
    // Some additional unnecessary steps
    removeDuplicates(data);
    quickSort(data);
}

// Good: Simple, efficient algorithm
void simpleSort(std::vector<int>& data) {
    std::sort(data.begin(), data.end());
}
```

In this example, the **simpleSort** function is more readable, and it uses the **efficient built-in std::sort** function without adding unnecessary steps that could complicate the algorithm.

3. Use Caching and Memoization

Instead of optimizing algorithms prematurely, consider **caching** results of expensive operations or using **memoization** to store previously computed results. This can yield significant

191

performance improvements while maintaining the original structure and readability of the code.

Example: Caching Results

cpp

```cpp
std::unordered_map<int, int> fib_cache;

int fib(int n) {
    if (n <= 1) return n;
    if (fib_cache.find(n) != fib_cache.end()) return fib_cache[n];
    fib_cache[n] = fib(n - 1) + fib(n - 2);
    return fib_cache[n];
}
```

In this example, memoization is used to optimize the Fibonacci sequence computation without altering the basic structure of the code or introducing unnecessary complexity.

Balancing Readability and Performance in Large Systems

In **large systems**, balancing performance and readability becomes even more critical. These systems are often complex and involve many interacting components, so finding the right balance will ensure that the system remains **efficient** while also being **maintainable**.

1. Design for Scalability First

Design the system to be scalable from the outset. This involves making trade-offs for **flexibility** and **maintainability**, such as using **modular architecture**, separating concerns, and writing clean interfaces. You can then **optimize specific parts** as needed, based on profiling and testing.

2. Code Reviews and Pair Programming

In large systems, **code reviews** and **pair programming** are valuable practices for maintaining the balance between performance and readability. Working with other developers helps ensure that the code remains clean, readable, and optimized only when necessary.

3. Use High-Level Frameworks

When appropriate, consider using high-level frameworks or libraries that are designed to handle common tasks efficiently. These frameworks often have built-in optimizations, so you don't need to focus on low-level performance tuning unless there is a specific bottleneck.

Case Studies of Optimizing Real-World Applications

1. Refactoring an E-Commerce Platform

An **e-commerce platform** with high traffic struggled with slow load times due to inefficient database queries and redundant processing during checkout. The team used profiling to identify the bottlenecks and optimized key queries.

Optimization Process:

- **Profiling** identified slow database queries and redundant calculations.
- They refactored the queries to be more efficient by using **indexing** and **query caching**.
- They optimized the checkout process by reducing the number of redundant calls to external services.
- Throughout the process, the code was kept simple and readable, ensuring that the optimizations didn't compromise future maintainability.

Outcome:

- The platform saw a **50% reduction** in load times and an improved user experience, all while maintaining a clean and understandable codebase.

194

2. Optimizing a Mobile App

A mobile app had performance issues, especially when loading large datasets. After profiling, the team identified that **image loading** and **database queries** were the main culprits.

Optimization Process:

- They used **lazy loading** for images, loading them only when needed.
- Database queries were optimized to return only the required data, reducing the amount of memory used.
- They used **background threading** for data processing to keep the UI responsive.

Outcome:

- The app became **more responsive**, and the number of crashes and performance issues decreased significantly, without sacrificing the simplicity and clarity of the code.

Conclusion

Striking the right balance between **performance** and **readability** is an essential skill for every software developer. While performance is crucial for building fast and efficient systems, it

195

should not come at the cost of readability, which ensures that the code is maintainable, understandable, and flexible. By focusing on **profiling, avoiding premature optimization**, and **writing clean, simple code**, developers can create high-performing applications without introducing unnecessary complexity. Case studies demonstrate how applying these principles in real-world projects leads to **robust, scalable**, and **maintainable** systems that deliver great performance without sacrificing clarity.

CHAPTER 15

SCALABILITY IN CLEAN CODE: WRITING FOR THE FUTURE

As software applications evolve, the need for **scalability** becomes increasingly critical. Writing code with scalability in mind ensures that your application can handle growth—whether it's an increase in user base, data, or new features—without becoming unwieldy or difficult to maintain. In this chapter, we will explore how to design code for **future growth**, how to write **modular**, **extensible** code that scales well, and how **design patterns** and **best practices** contribute to building scalable systems. We will also look at an example of scaling a **small application** to an **enterprise-level system** to see how scalability principles are applied in real-world scenarios.

Designing Code for Future Growth

When you write code for scalability, you're designing it not only for the current requirements but also for the anticipated future needs. **Future growth** might involve handling **more data**, **more users**, or **more features**, but if the code isn't built with flexibility and adaptability in mind, scaling becomes an expensive and time-consuming process. The key to scaling is **anticipation**— designing code that can accommodate change and growth over time without requiring a complete rewrite.

1. Anticipate Changes Early

Consider how the system may evolve over time and structure your code to accommodate those changes without significant refactoring. **Modular architecture**, **separation of concerns**, and **loose coupling** are strategies that ensure your code can grow without being brittle.

Example:

Imagine you're building a **user management system**. Initially, your system might only need to handle basic user data (e.g., name, email, password). However, over time, you may need to handle more complex requirements, like user roles, permissions, and even third-party integrations. By creating a **modular system** that can easily extend and integrate with external services, you future-proof the application.

2. Prioritize Flexibility and Extensibility

When designing for scalability, the system should be able to handle **future requirements** without major rewrites. **Extensibility** allows for new functionality to be added easily as the project evolves.

- **Use interfaces and abstract classes** to define clear, adaptable contracts between different parts of the system.
- **Design for reusability**: Create components that can be reused across different parts of the application or even in different projects.

Example: Designing for Extensibility

Suppose you have a **payment processing** system. Initially, you might support only one payment provider, but in the future, you may need to support others. By designing your payment system with interfaces like `IPaymentProvider` and implementing the `PaymentProcessor` to interact with these interfaces, you can add new payment providers without changing the core logic.

cpp

```cpp
class IPaymentProvider {
public:
    virtual void processPayment(double amount) =
0;
};

class PayPalProvider : public IPaymentProvider {
public:
    void processPayment(double amount) override
{
        // PayPal payment processing logic
```

```cpp
    }
};


class StripeProvider : public IPaymentProvider {
public:
    void processPayment(double amount) override
{
        // Stripe payment processing logic
    }
};


class PaymentProcessor {
private:
    IPaymentProvider* provider;
public:
    PaymentProcessor(IPaymentProvider* provider)
: provider(provider) {}

    void process(double amount) {
        provider->processPayment(amount);
    }
};
```

In this example, the `PaymentProcessor` is designed to easily support multiple providers, making the code extensible and adaptable to future changes.

Writing Modular, Extensible Code That Can Scale

Modular code is code that is divided into **small, manageable pieces** with clearly defined responsibilities. **Modularization** helps make the system easier to understand, test, and maintain, which is essential when scaling a system. As the application grows, these modular pieces can be extended or replaced without affecting other parts of the code.

1. Emphasize Separation of Concerns

Each module or class should have a **single responsibility**, which is a core principle of clean, scalable design. This prevents the system from becoming tightly coupled and reduces the impact of changes in one area on other parts of the system.

Example: Separation of Concerns

If you are building a **content management system (CMS)**, separate the logic for managing content from the logic for managing users. This way, each module can evolve independently.

- **Content Management Module**: Handles creating, updating, and deleting content.
- **User Management Module**: Handles authentication, permissions, and user roles.

By keeping these concerns separate, you ensure that modifications in one area (e.g., adding new content types) do not impact other areas (e.g., user management).

2. Use Design Patterns for Scalability

Design patterns are proven solutions to common software design problems. By applying the right design patterns, you can create scalable systems that are easier to maintain.

- **Factory Pattern**: Useful for creating instances of classes without tightly coupling the client to the concrete class.
- **Singleton Pattern**: Ensures that a class has only one instance, useful for global objects like database connections.
- **Observer Pattern**: Useful for implementing event-driven architectures where components must be notified of changes.

Example: Using the Factory Pattern

Suppose you're building a **report generation system**. You might need to generate different types of reports (PDF, Excel, HTML). The **Factory Pattern** can help create report objects without tightly coupling the code to specific report types.

cpp

```cpp
class IReport {
public:
    virtual void generateReport() = 0;
};

class PDFReport : public IReport {
public:
    void generateReport() override {
        std::cout << "Generating PDF report..." << std::endl;
    }
};

class ExcelReport : public IReport {
public:
    void generateReport() override {
        std::cout << "Generating Excel report..." << std::endl;
    }
};

class ReportFactory {
public:
    static IReport* createReport(const std::string& type) {
        if (type == "pdf") {
            return new PDFReport();
        } else if (type == "excel") {
            return new ExcelReport();
```

```
    }
    return nullptr;
  }
};


// Client code
IReport*                report              =
ReportFactory::createReport("pdf");
report->generateReport();
```

In this case, the Factory Pattern helps decouple the code that uses reports from the specific types of reports, making it easier to extend the system with new report types in the future.

The Role of Patterns and Practices in Scalable Architecture

Patterns and best practices are crucial in building systems that can scale. By using **architectural patterns** such as **microservices** or **event-driven architectures**, you can create systems that are **highly available**, **fault-tolerant**, and able to handle growth in terms of traffic, data, and complexity.

204

1. Microservices Architecture

A **microservices architecture** breaks down a system into smaller, independent services, each responsible for a specific task or domain. This approach enhances scalability because each service can be scaled independently based on demand.

Benefits of Microservices:

- **Scalability**: Each service can be scaled independently, reducing the need to scale the entire system.
- **Flexibility**: Different services can use different technologies, allowing the system to evolve more easily.
- **Fault Tolerance**: If one service fails, the others can continue to function, increasing system resilience.

2. Event-Driven Architecture

An **event-driven architecture** is based on the concept of **events**—things that happen within the system that need to be processed. This allows for **asynchronous communication** and helps scale systems without creating bottlenecks.

Benefits of Event-Driven Architecture:

- **Decoupling**: Components can communicate without needing to know about each other directly.

- **Scalability**: Services can consume events in parallel, improving throughput and performance.

Example of Scaling a Small Application to an Enterprise-Level System

Let's consider an example of scaling a **small task management application** to an **enterprise-level system**.

1. Initial Small-Scale Design

In the initial version of the task management application, the system might be built with a **monolithic architecture**, where a single database and service handle all requests. While this works for a small user base, the system starts to face performance issues as more users, tasks, and features are added.

2. Transition to Microservices

As the application scales, it is refactored to a **microservices architecture**. Different services are created for **user management, task management, notifications**, and **report generation**. These services communicate via APIs or message queues, and each service can be scaled independently.

3. Adding Event-Driven Components

To handle notifications and messaging in real-time, the system is updated to use an **event-driven architecture**. When a task is created, an event is fired, and the notification service listens for that event to send notifications to users.

4. Distributed Databases

As the system grows, the monolithic database is replaced with **distributed databases** that allow for **sharding** and **replication**, improving both performance and availability.

5. CI/CD and Automated Testing

To ensure the system remains reliable as it scales, **Continuous Integration** and **Continuous Deployment (CI/CD)** practices are implemented, alongside extensive **automated testing**.

Outcome:

By applying these practices and patterns, the task management application is able to handle **millions of users**, process large amounts of data, and scale dynamically based on traffic demands, all while maintaining a **clean**, **modular**, and **extensible** architecture.

Conclusion

Designing scalable systems requires **careful planning** and **architectural foresight**. By designing code with **future growth** in mind, writing **modular, extensible** code, and using proven **patterns** and **best practices**, you can create applications that scale effectively without sacrificing clarity or maintainability. The examples and case studies discussed in this chapter demonstrate how scalability can be achieved in real-world systems, whether through **microservices, event-driven architectures**, or **distributed systems**. By following these principles, you can ensure that your application will continue to perform well as it grows and evolves over time.

CHAPTER 16

DESIGNING FOR TESTABILITY

Writing **testable code** is an essential aspect of building reliable and maintainable software. Designing systems with **testability** in mind ensures that you can easily verify the correctness of your code and catch bugs early in the development process. This chapter explores how to write clean code that is easy to test, the importance of testability in software design, and practical techniques like **dependency injection** and **mocking** that make testing easier. We will also explore real-world examples of testable designs and systems that can be easily verified and extended.

Writing Clean Code That Is Easy to Test

To design code that is easy to test, we must prioritize the following principles:

1. Modular Code Design

Modularity is the cornerstone of **testable code**. By breaking the system into small, independent units (such as **functions**, **classes**, and **modules**), you can more easily isolate the parts of the system that need to be tested.

- **Single Responsibility Principle (SRP)**: Each function or class should have a single responsibility. This makes it easier to understand and test.
- **Loose Coupling**: Minimize dependencies between modules, as tightly coupled systems are harder to test. A system where components are **independent** of each other is easier to isolate for testing.

Example: Refactoring a Complex Function

Before:

cpp

```
void      processOrder(int      orderId,      bool
applyDiscount) {
    // Fetch order from database
    // Calculate total
    // Apply discount
    // Update inventory
}
```

This function is doing too many things and is difficult to test, as it involves **database access, business logic**, and **external systems**.

After:

210

cpp

```cpp
class OrderProcessor {
public:
    double calculateTotal(int orderId);
    void applyDiscount(Order& order, bool
applyDiscount);
    void updateInventory(Order& order);
};
```

Now, each function is focused on a **single responsibility**, making it easier to write isolated tests for each part of the system.

2. Clear Separation of Concerns

The **Separation of Concerns (SoC)** principle helps keep different responsibilities in separate classes or modules, making them easier to test in isolation.

- **Business Logic**: Should be contained in **services** or **managers** that can be easily tested.
- **UI and Data Access Logic**: Should be isolated so that you can test the business logic without involving databases or UI elements.

By decoupling business logic from other concerns (like **UI rendering** or **database access**), you can test the core functionality independently.

211

The Importance of Designing Code with Testability in Mind

Testability should be a key consideration **from the start** of the design process. If the system is designed with testability in mind, it becomes easier to ensure that the software behaves as expected through automated tests.

1. Testable Code Is Reliable Code

Testable code tends to be more **reliable** because it allows you to catch bugs early, maintain consistent functionality, and prevent regressions as the codebase grows.

2. Easier Maintenance and Refactoring

When you write code with testability in mind, you ensure that changes and **refactorings** don't break existing functionality. A strong suite of **unit tests** allows developers to modify and improve the codebase with confidence.

3. Encourages Simpler, Focused Code

Testable code naturally leads to simpler, **focused designs**. Since each unit or module can be tested independently, there's less need

212

for unnecessary complexity or interdependencies. This promotes a cleaner and easier-to-understand codebase.

Dependency Injection and Mocking in Test-Driven Environments

In test-driven development (TDD) and unit testing environments, **dependency injection** and **mocking** are powerful tools that make it easier to isolate units of code and test them independently.

1. Dependency Injection (DI)

Dependency Injection is a technique where **dependencies** (objects or services that a class needs to function) are passed into the class, rather than being created inside it. This makes the class **decoupled** from its dependencies, making it easier to **mock** or **stub** them during testing.

Why Dependency Injection Helps Testability:

- **Separation of Concerns**: It allows you to separate the core logic of a class from the components it depends on, such as **databases, third-party services**, or **external APIs**.

- **Test Isolation**: DI allows you to pass in mock or fake dependencies during tests, which lets you isolate the functionality you're testing from external factors.

Example: Using Dependency Injection

cpp

```cpp
class OrderService {
private:
    PaymentProcessor* paymentProcessor;
public:
    // Constructor injection
    OrderService(PaymentProcessor* processor) :
paymentProcessor(processor) {}

    void processOrder(Order& order) {
        // Process payment using the injected
dependency
        paymentProcessor-
>processPayment(order.getTotalAmount());
    }
};
```

In this example, OrderService depends on PaymentProcessor, but instead of creating the PaymentProcessor inside OrderService, we **inject** it via the constructor. This makes it easier to test OrderService by passing in a **mock PaymentProcessor** during testing.

214

2. Mocking

Mocking is the process of simulating real objects (like databases or external APIs) in tests. By using mock objects, you can **simulate dependencies** and **control their behavior** during testing, ensuring that your tests remain **isolated** and independent.

Mocking with a Framework (e.g., Google Mock):

cpp

```cpp
#include <gmock/gmock.h>

class MockPaymentProcessor : public PaymentProcessor {
public:
    MOCK_METHOD(void, processPayment, (double amount), (override));
};

void testProcessOrder() {
    MockPaymentProcessor mockProcessor;
    OrderService orderService(&mockProcessor);

    EXPECT_CALL(mockProcessor, processPayment(100.0));

    Order order;
    order.setTotalAmount(100.0);
```

215

```
orderService.processOrder(order);  // Verify
processPayment was called
}
```

In this test, we use **Google Mock** to create a mock
`PaymentProcessor`, allowing us to verify that the
`processPayment` method is called without needing a real
payment processor.

Real-World Examples of Testable Designs and Systems

1. Testable API Design

Imagine you're building an API for **user management**. The
design involves interacting with the database to create, update, and
delete user accounts. To make this system testable, we isolate the
logic that interacts with the database from the business logic and
inject it into the controller or service.

Example of a Testable API Design:
cpp

```
class UserService {
private:
    UserRepository* repository;
```

```cpp
public:
    UserService(UserRepository*    repo)    :
repository(repo) {}

    User        createUser(std::string        name,
std::string email) {
        if (repository->existsByEmail(email)) {
            throw    std::invalid_argument("Email
already in use");
        }
        return        repository->save(User(name,
email));
    }
};
```

By injecting the UserRepository as a dependency, we can easily mock the repository during unit tests, ensuring that we can test the **business logic** without depending on the database.

Unit Test Example:

cpp

```cpp
void testCreateUser() {
    MockUserRepository mockRepo;
    UserService userService(&mockRepo);

    EXPECT_CALL(mockRepo,
existsByEmail("test@example.com"))
        .WillOnce(Return(false));
```

```
EXPECT_CALL(mockRepo, save(testing::_));

    User   user  =   userService.createUser("John
Doe", "test@example.com");
}
```

In this test, we use **mocking** to simulate the behavior of the `UserRepository`, allowing us to isolate and test the business logic in the `UserService`.

2. Testable Microservices

In a microservice architecture, each microservice should be designed to be **testable in isolation**. This is typically achieved by making services **stateless**, **modular**, and **loosely coupled**.

Example of Testable Microservices:

Consider an **order service** in an e-commerce system. It might interact with other services like **inventory management** and **payment processing**. To make the `OrderService` testable, it should use **dependency injection** for both the payment and inventory services.

cpp

```
class OrderService {
private:
    InventoryService* inventory;
```

```
    PaymentService* payment;
public:
    OrderService(InventoryService*      inventory,
PaymentService* payment)
        : inventory(inventory), payment(payment)
{}


    bool placeOrder(Order& order) {
        if                        (!inventory-
>isAvailable(order.getProductId())) {
            throw std::out_of_stock_exception();
        }
        if                          (payment-
>processPayment(order.getTotalAmount())) {
            inventory-
>updateStock(order.getProductId(),
order.getQuantity());
            return true;
        }
        return false;
    }
};
```

Here, both `InventoryService` and `PaymentService` are injected as dependencies, making it easy to **mock** these services in tests.

Unit Test Example:

cpp

```
void testPlaceOrder() {
    MockInventoryService mockInventory;
    MockPaymentService mockPayment;
    OrderService    orderService(&mockInventory,
&mockPayment);

    EXPECT_CALL(mockInventory, isAvailable(1))
        .WillOnce(Return(true));
    EXPECT_CALL(mockPayment,
processPayment(100.0))
        .WillOnce(Return(true));

    Order order;
    order.setProductId(1);
    order.setQuantity(2);
    order.setTotalAmount(100.0);

    bool                result            =
orderService.placeOrder(order);
    ASSERT_TRUE(result);
}
```

This test verifies the behavior of the OrderService without depending on the actual implementation of the InventoryService or PaymentService.

Conclusion

Designing software for testability is crucial for building **robust**, **maintainable**, and **reliable** applications. By writing **modular code**, adhering to principles like **dependency injection**, and utilizing **mocking** frameworks, you can ensure that your system is **easy to test** and **scale**. Testable systems are not only easier to validate, but they also enable you to **refactor** and **evolve** the code without breaking functionality. Real-world examples show that testable designs are not just a theoretical practice; they have tangible benefits in ensuring that software is always in a verified, working state throughout its lifecycle.

CHAPTER 17

CODE REVIEWS: THE KEY TO CONTINUOUS IMPROVEMENT

Code reviews are one of the most effective ways to ensure **clean code**, promote **best practices**, and maintain **high-quality software**. They not only help identify bugs and inconsistencies but also foster a culture of continuous improvement within development teams. By involving multiple developers in the review process, the likelihood of catching issues early increases, and the overall quality of the software is significantly enhanced. This chapter delves into the **value** of code reviews, **how to conduct an effective code review**, the **importance of constructive feedback**, and **how to build a culture of code quality** within teams. Additionally, we'll look at **real-world case studies** where successful code review processes led to improved code quality.

The Value of Code Reviews in Maintaining Clean Code

Code reviews play a **crucial role** in ensuring that code remains clean, maintainable, and scalable. They are a valuable tool for spotting potential problems early and ensuring that the code adheres to project standards.

1. Ensuring Consistency

Code reviews help ensure that the codebase follows consistent **coding standards**. This includes everything from **naming conventions** to **indentation** and **function design**. Consistency across the codebase improves **readability**, making it easier for developers to understand and modify the code.

2. Identifying Bugs and Issues Early

Reviews allow for early detection of bugs, performance problems, or design flaws that might have been overlooked by the author. Catching these issues early in the process, before they reach production, reduces the cost and effort needed to fix them later.

3. Promoting Best Practices

Through code reviews, team members can **learn from each other** and enforce **best practices**. They provide an opportunity to discuss why certain design patterns or strategies are preferred, allowing developers to improve their skills over time.

4. Encouraging Knowledge Sharing

Code reviews promote **cross-team knowledge sharing**. They help ensure that developers understand different parts of the application, which is particularly useful for maintaining large codebases or during team transitions. By reviewing each other's code, team members are exposed to different approaches and solutions, improving their overall coding skills.

How to Conduct an Effective Code Review

To get the most out of code reviews, it's essential to approach them in a structured, efficient manner. A poorly conducted review can lead to confusion, frustration, and missed opportunities to improve the code.

1. Establish Clear Objectives

Before starting a code review, establish what you want to achieve. Key objectives often include:

- Ensuring the code **meets functional requirements**.
- Verifying that it follows **coding standards**.
- Ensuring that it is **efficient** and **maintainable**.
- Identifying potential bugs and areas for optimization.

224

2. Prepare the Code for Review

Before submitting code for review, ensure it is:

- **Clean and organized**: Avoid submitting unfinished work.
- **Well-documented**: Include comments where necessary, especially if the logic is complex or unconventional.
- **Unit tested**: Ensure the code has been tested thoroughly, and provide the unit tests to facilitate the review process.

3. Conduct the Review

When reviewing code, focus on the following aspects:

- **Readability**: Is the code easy to understand? Are the names of variables and functions clear and descriptive? Can someone unfamiliar with the codebase understand the logic?
- **Correctness**: Does the code perform as expected? Are there edge cases that haven't been accounted for?
- **Efficiency**: Is the code efficient in terms of memory and CPU usage? Are there any unnecessary operations?
- **Maintainability**: Is the code modular? Can it be easily updated or extended in the future?

4. Provide Actionable Feedback

When providing feedback, ensure that it is:

- **Specific**: Point out exact lines of code and explain why they need improvement.
- **Constructive**: Focus on providing solutions and alternatives rather than just pointing out issues.
- **Objective**: Keep the discussion focused on the code, not on the person who wrote it.

5. Allow Time for Follow-up

Give the original author time to make changes and respond to feedback. Follow up to ensure that the code has been revised according to the suggestions and that any issues have been resolved.

Giving and Receiving Constructive Feedback

Effective code reviews depend on **constructive feedback**. It is crucial that feedback is clear, actionable, and aimed at improving the code, rather than criticizing the developer. Here's how to give and receive feedback constructively:

1. Giving Constructive Feedback

- **Be Respectful and Professional**: Code reviews should be collaborative, not adversarial. Avoid negative language or personal criticism. Focus on improving the code, not criticizing the individual.
- **Be Specific**: Point out exactly where the code needs improvement and why. Provide specific examples of better alternatives.
- **Encourage Growth**: When you notice areas where the developer can improve, provide guidance on how they can learn or do better in the future. For example, "Consider using a more descriptive variable name here" or "This function can be simplified by using a helper method."

Example of Constructive Feedback:

- **Instead of**: "This code is confusing."
- **Try**: "This function is a bit difficult to follow. Consider breaking it down into smaller, more focused functions to improve readability."

2. Receiving Constructive Feedback

Receiving feedback can sometimes be challenging, but it's an essential part of **continuous improvement**. Here's how to handle it positively:

- **Stay Open-Minded**: Listen to the feedback without getting defensive. Remember, the goal is to improve the code and learn.
- **Ask for Clarification**: If feedback is unclear, don't hesitate to ask for specific examples or suggestions.
- **Act on Feedback**: Make changes to the code based on the feedback provided. If you disagree with the feedback, provide your reasoning and be open to further discussion.

Building a Culture of Code Quality in Teams

Creating a **culture of code quality** within a team is key to maintaining clean, reliable software. Code reviews are a critical part of this culture, but they should be supported by other practices and an environment that encourages continuous improvement.

1. Encourage Team Collaboration

Create an atmosphere where developers collaborate, share knowledge, and provide constructive feedback. Encourage team members to participate in code reviews, and provide opportunities for learning and improvement.

2. Promote Code Ownership

Encourage a sense of **ownership** of the code. When developers take ownership of their code, they are more likely to write high-quality, well-tested software and embrace feedback to make improvements.

3. Set Clear Coding Standards

Ensure that your team adheres to **coding standards** and **best practices**. This could include guidelines for code formatting, naming conventions, and documentation practices. Consistent code across the team makes reviews easier and more productive.

4. Make Code Reviews Regular

Integrate code reviews into your **development workflow**. Make them a regular, essential part of the process rather than an afterthought. Set aside time each day or week for code reviews to ensure they're consistent and effective.

5. Use Tools to Facilitate Code Reviews

Take advantage of code review tools like **GitHub Pull Requests**, **GitLab Merge Requests**, **Crucible**, or **Phabricator**. These tools make it easy to review code, leave comments, and track changes.

Case Studies of Successful Code Review Processes

1. Large-Scale Web Application – E-commerce Platform

In a large-scale **e-commerce platform**, the development team implemented a **peer review** system where every piece of code was reviewed before it was merged into the main codebase. They focused on readability, performance, and scalability in their reviews.

Impact:

- The process led to **fewer bugs** in production and higher quality code overall.
- Developers learned from each other's suggestions, improving their coding practices over time.
- The team was able to maintain a **high standard of code quality** as the codebase grew in size.

2. Enterprise-Grade Mobile App – Fintech Application

In a **fintech mobile application**, the team integrated **automated static analysis** tools and **manual code reviews** into their development process. They focused on **security** and **compliance** during their code reviews to ensure the application was secure and met regulatory requirements.

Impact:

- **Security vulnerabilities** were identified early in the development process, and the team was able to resolve them before they became a serious issue.
- The team built a **shared knowledge base** around security best practices and incorporated it into the code review process, ensuring that new features followed the same rigorous standards.

3. Open-Source Project – Data Analytics Library

In an **open-source data analytics library**, contributors from around the world engaged in code reviews through **GitHub Pull Requests**. The project maintained a strong focus on **maintainability** and **test coverage**.

Impact:

- **Collaboration** between contributors improved, with feedback from more experienced developers helping newer contributors improve their skills.
- The code review process ensured that the library was **extensible** and **easy to maintain** as new features were added.
- The project gained a **reputation for quality** due to the rigor of the review process.

231

Conclusion

Code reviews are an essential part of maintaining **clean code** and ensuring **continuous improvement** in software development. They foster a culture of collaboration, knowledge sharing, and high standards. By conducting effective reviews, giving and receiving constructive feedback, and promoting code quality, development teams can consistently produce high-quality software. Real-world case studies show how well-structured code review processes contribute to the long-term success and maintainability of software projects, whether in enterprise systems, open-source projects, or large-scale applications.

CHAPTER 18

VERSION CONTROL: KEEPING CLEAN CODE IN CHECK

Version control is an essential tool for maintaining clean code, enabling **collaboration, trackability**, and **efficiency** in software development. With version control systems (VCS) like **Git**, developers can ensure that the codebase remains **organized, coherent**, and **easily manageable**. Version control helps prevent chaos, particularly in teams where multiple developers are working on the same project. This chapter explores the **importance of version control**, best practices for **branching strategies**, how to **write meaningful commit messages**, and real-world examples of how **clean version control practices** can maintain a well-organized and maintainable codebase.

The Importance of Using Version Control Systems (VCS) for Clean Code Management

A **version control system (VCS)** helps developers track changes in the codebase over time. It acts as a **repository** for the project's history, allowing developers to manage and revert changes, collaborate with other developers, and ensure that the code remains clean and stable. **Git**, as the most widely used VCS, provides features like **branching**, **merging**, and **commit history**, all of which support clean code practices.

1. Enables Collaboration

In a collaborative development environment, multiple developers might work on different parts of the code simultaneously. Version control systems allow **concurrent changes** without the risk of overwriting each other's work. **Git** provides features like **branching**, allowing developers to work independently on different features without interfering with the main project.

2. Tracks Changes Over Time

With version control, you can track every change made to the codebase, including additions, deletions, and modifications. This is crucial for maintaining clean code, as it allows you to **roll back** to a previous state if a mistake is made, ensuring that the codebase remains in a consistent and working state.

3. Prevents Code Loss

Version control serves as a **backup** for your code. Even if you make a mistake, the ability to check out previous versions of your code provides an **insurance policy** against accidental loss. This promotes experimentation and iterative development while ensuring that developers can always recover lost work.

4. Facilitates Code Review and Quality Control

Version control makes it easier to conduct **code reviews**, where team members review each other's changes before merging them into the main codebase. This helps ensure that only **clean, well-structured**, and **tested** code makes it to production.

Branching Strategies for Maintainable Codebases

A well-thought-out branching strategy is vital for maintaining a clean and scalable codebase. **Git** enables developers to create **branches** for features, bug fixes, or experiments without affecting the main codebase (usually called the **master** or **main** branch). The key to an effective version control system is using the right branching strategy to ensure that the codebase remains organized, maintainable, and free from conflicts.

1. Feature Branching

Feature branching is a strategy where each new feature or bug fix is developed in its own **branch**, separate from the main codebase. This allows developers to work independently without disrupting the stability of the main branch.

Workflow:

- Create a new branch for each feature: `git checkout -b feature/feature-name`
- Develop the feature independently in its branch.
- Once the feature is complete and tested, merge it into the main branch.

This approach helps keep the main codebase **stable** and free from incomplete or untested features.

2. Git Flow

The **Git Flow** model is a branching strategy that defines a set of rules for managing the branches of a project. It is particularly useful for larger teams and projects with defined **release cycles**.

Key Branches in Git Flow:

- **Main**: The stable, production-ready branch.
- **Develop**: The main branch where the latest development happens. This serves as the integration branch for features.
- **Feature**: Each new feature is developed in its own branch created from `develop`.
- **Release**: Before a new version is released, a release branch is created from `develop` for final testing and bug fixing.

236

- **Hotfix**: Emergency fixes are made in `hotfix` branches, which are created from `main` and merged back into both `main` and `develop`.

This structured branching strategy ensures that releases are **well-managed**, and emergency fixes can be applied without disrupting ongoing feature development.

3. Trunk-Based Development

In **trunk-based development**, all developers work directly in the **main branch** (referred to as the **trunk**). However, they create **short-lived feature branches** that are merged back into the main branch frequently, often multiple times a day.

Advantages:

- Keeps the main branch always in a **deployable** state.
- Allows for **continuous integration** and regular testing.
- Reduces the chances of **merge conflicts** by ensuring that changes are integrated quickly.

This strategy works best for teams practicing **continuous integration/continuous delivery (CI/CD)**.

Keeping Commit Messages Meaningful and Clear

Commit messages are an essential part of **version control** because they serve as the documentation of the changes made to the codebase. Well-written commit messages help developers understand the history of the project, track bugs, and review changes. **Meaningful commit messages** are crucial for maintaining clean code because they provide context for future developers and make it easier to understand why certain changes were made.

1. Structure of a Good Commit Message

A good commit message typically consists of:

- **Title (Summary)**: A concise summary of what the commit does. Keep it under **50 characters**.
- **Body (Detailed Description)**: A more detailed explanation of the changes, why they were made, and how they solve the problem.
- **Footer (Optional)**: References to issues or pull requests related to the commit.

Example:

pgsql

```
Fix bug in order processing that prevents
shipping calculation
```

```
- Corrected logic that was skipping shipping cost
calculation for orders
  with special discounts.
- Updated unit tests to cover edge cases for
shipping.
```

This commit message is clear, specific, and provides context about the changes made. It also includes details about the **problem** and the **solution**.

2. Follow Consistent Message Guidelines

To maintain a clean and understandable history of commits, it's important to follow a consistent format for commit messages. Teams should agree on guidelines that cover:

- The **style** and **structure** of commit messages (e.g., whether to use present or past tense).
- Whether to include **issue IDs** or **references to pull requests** in the commit messages.

This consistency helps ensure that the history remains **clear** and **easy to navigate**.

Real-World Examples of Clean Version Control Practices

1. Open-Source Project – Web Framework

In an open-source project, the developers use a **Git flow** branching strategy to manage new features, hotfixes, and releases. They consistently use **meaningful commit messages** and create a **release branch** before every major release.

Impact:

- The project has **well-maintained release cycles** and **separation of concerns** between development, testing, and production environments.
- The commit history is clear, and every change is documented, making it easier for contributors to understand the evolution of the code.

2. Large-Scale Enterprise Application – E-Commerce Platform

An e-commerce platform with multiple teams working on different features uses **feature branches** and **pull requests** for all code changes. Every developer submits a pull request that undergoes **peer reviews** before being merged into the main branch.

Impact:

- The code is **modular**, and each feature is developed in isolation, reducing the risk of conflicts.

240

- Pull requests are reviewed for **readability**, **correctness**, and adherence to coding standards, ensuring that only clean code is merged into the main branch.

3. CI/CD Pipeline – Cloud-Based Application

In a cloud-based application, the team uses **trunk-based development** with **continuous integration** to ensure that the main branch is always in a deployable state. Developers commit small changes to the main branch multiple times a day, triggering **automated tests** and **deployment pipelines**.

Impact:

- The application is always **deployable**, reducing the time between code changes and production deployment.
- Developers can quickly **fix issues** as they arise, maintaining a fast-paced, efficient development cycle without sacrificing code quality.

Conclusion

Version control is a fundamental tool for maintaining clean, maintainable, and scalable codebases. By following best practices like using structured branching strategies, writing meaningful commit messages, and consistently using version control systems like **Git**, development teams can ensure that the code remains organized, stable, and easy to manage. Real-world examples show how clean version control practices contribute to the success of both large-scale enterprise applications and collaborative open-source projects. With effective version control, teams can foster collaboration, ensure code quality, and streamline the development process, ultimately leading to better software and more efficient workflows.

CHAPTER 19

DESIGNING CLEAN APIS

APIs (Application Programming Interfaces) are the backbone of many modern software systems, enabling communication between different services, applications, and components. A **clean API** is easy to understand, intuitive to use, and maintainable over time. This chapter explores **principles for writing clean, intuitive APIs**, the importance of **versioning APIs** without breaking existing clients, and how to keep APIs **simple** and **easy to use**. We will also look at **real-world examples** of both clean and poorly designed APIs to highlight the dos and don'ts of API design.

Principles for Writing Clean, Intuitive APIs

A clean API is designed with its **users** (developers who consume the API) in mind. It should be **easy to understand**, **easy to integrate**, and **consistent**. The following principles can guide you in creating a well-designed API:

1. Consistency

A clean API should follow **consistent conventions**. From **naming** to **method signatures**, consistency makes it easier for developers to use your API without having to constantly refer to documentation. Adhering to consistent patterns helps ensure that once developers understand one part of the API, they can confidently use others.

- **Naming Conventions**: Use **descriptive names** for your methods, classes, and parameters. For example, if you have a method that retrieves an item by ID, name it `getItemById` instead of something vague like `getData`.

2. Intuitiveness

An intuitive API is one that **just makes sense**. It should align with **common patterns** and conventions that developers are familiar with. Developers should be able to predict the behavior of an API based on prior experience.

Best Practices for Intuitive APIs:

- Keep method names **short** but **descriptive**. Avoid unnecessary verbosity.
- Organize your API logically. Group related functions together.

244

- Make your API feel familiar to users by adhering to industry-standard practices (e.g., **RESTful principles** for web APIs, **CamelCase** for naming conventions).

3. Minimizing Surprises

A clean API avoids **unexpected behavior**. If an API does something unexpected or behaves inconsistently, it will confuse users and lead to bugs.

- **Clear error handling**: Provide **clear error messages** and status codes. If something goes wrong, make sure the API provides a helpful response that makes it easy for developers to troubleshoot.
- Avoid **side effects** that are not well-documented. Changes to state or behavior should be predictable and not hidden in the implementation.

4. Simplicity

Keep it simple. Avoid **over-engineering** the API by introducing unnecessary complexity. An API should expose only what is necessary for the consumer to interact with, and hide implementation details.

- **Minimalism**: Provide only the **essential features**. Don't add features just because you can; instead, focus on delivering high-quality, well-designed functionality.

- **Fluent Design**: When designing an API, think about how the code will flow for users. The API should be **easy to use** and chainable, allowing for smooth integration into their codebase.

Versioning APIs Without Breaking Existing Clients

API versioning is crucial to maintaining a **backward-compatible** system, especially when new features are added or breaking changes are required. A well-versioned API ensures that **existing clients** continue to work even after updates, while new users can access the latest features.

1. Semantic Versioning (SemVer)

Semantic Versioning is a popular approach to API versioning. The format is MAJOR.MINOR.PATCH:

- **MAJOR**: Incremented when there are breaking changes.
- **MINOR**: Incremented when new features are added in a backward-compatible manner.
- **PATCH**: Incremented when bug fixes or small improvements are made.

Example:

- **1.0.0**: Initial version.
- **1.1.0**: New features added, no breaking changes.
- **2.0.0**: Major breaking changes that are incompatible with previous versions.

2. Versioning Strategies

There are several ways to handle API versioning:

- **URI Versioning (Path Versioning)**: Including the version number in the URL path.
  - Example: `https://api.example.com/v1/`
- **Query Parameter Versioning**: Including the version as a query parameter.
  - Example:
    `https://api.example.com/items?version=1`
- **Header Versioning**: Versioning through custom request headers.
  - Example: Add `Accept: application/vnd.example.v1+json` in the request header.

3. Deprecated Features

When removing or changing a feature, it's important to communicate it clearly and provide a **deprecation notice**. Offer **alternative solutions** and give clients enough time to migrate to the new version without disrupting their workflow.

Example of Deprecation Notice:

- **"The `getUserByEmail` method is deprecated and will be removed in v3.0.0. Please use the `getUserById` method instead."**

Keeping APIs Simple and Easy to Use

Simplicity is key when designing APIs. A simple API is **easier to integrate**, **faster to learn**, and **less prone to bugs**. Here are some guidelines for keeping your API simple:

1. Avoid Unnecessary Features

Don't overcomplicate your API by adding features that aren't necessary for the core functionality. Keep the API focused on the **primary use cases** and only expose what's needed for the consumers to achieve their goals.

2. Provide Defaults and Reasonable Assumptions

Where possible, make **reasonable assumptions** and provide **default values** that minimize the need for the consumer to specify every detail. This reduces friction for users and makes the API easier to use.

Example:

If a user is submitting a request for an item and doesn't provide a filter or sorting option, the API should return results in a **reasonable default order**, rather than failing with an error.

3. Minimize Dependencies

Minimize external dependencies within your API. This reduces the complexity of integrating the API into different systems and ensures it remains maintainable over time.

4. Document Clearly

Clear and thorough documentation is crucial for usability. **Good documentation** reduces the learning curve and makes the API easier to adopt. Provide **examples** and **edge cases** to help users understand the API's behavior.

Examples of Clean APIs and Poorly Designed APIs

Clean API Example: Stripe API

Stripe's API is a great example of a clean, well-designed API. It follows **RESTful principles** and is **easy to use** with clear documentation.

- **Intuitive naming**: Endpoints like `/charges`, `/customers`, `/payments` are straightforward and descriptive.
- **Consistent behavior**: All endpoints follow consistent conventions, including error handling, data formats, and responses.
- **Versioning**: Stripe uses **versioning in headers**, which allows them to introduce new features while keeping backward compatibility for existing clients.

Example Request:

bash

```
POST https://api.stripe.com/v1/charges
```

Stripe's API provides comprehensive documentation, making it easy for developers to integrate payment processing into their applications.

Poor API Example: Overly Complex, Unintuitive API

Consider an API with endpoints like `/doSomething?param1=5&param2=hello` where the purpose of the endpoint is unclear, and the parameters are cryptic and not well-documented. Additionally, the responses from the API contain inconsistent naming conventions, and the versioning is handled through a confusing combination of query parameters and headers.

- **Unclear endpoint names**: The endpoint does not convey any meaningful information about its functionality.
- **Non-descriptive parameters**: Parameters like `param1` and `param2` don't explain their purpose, making the API difficult to use.
- **Inconsistent error handling**: Different endpoints return errors in different formats, which leads to confusion for developers using the API.

Such an API would likely confuse developers and result in longer integration times, making the system **harder to maintain** and **more prone to errors**.

Conclusion

Designing clean, intuitive APIs is essential for building **easy-to-use**, **maintainable**, and **scalable** software systems. By adhering to best practices like **consistent naming conventions**, **intuitive structure**, **versioning strategies**, and **clear documentation**, you can ensure that your API remains clean and accessible to developers. Real-world examples show the importance of simplicity and clarity, highlighting how well-designed APIs, like Stripe's, provide an excellent user experience while maintaining robustness and flexibility. On the other hand, poorly designed APIs lead to confusion, frustration, and integration problems. By following the principles outlined in this chapter, you can create APIs that are both **clean** and **powerful**, making it easier for developers to integrate and work with your software.

CHAPTER 20

DOCUMENTATION: THE BACKBONE OF CLEAN CODE

In software development, **documentation** is an essential aspect of maintaining clean code. Good documentation not only helps developers understand how to use your code but also serves as a critical reference point for future development, debugging, and onboarding new team members. This chapter will delve into **best practices** for writing **clear, concise,** and **helpful documentation** that enhances the maintainability of the codebase. We will explore the role of **docstrings, comments,** and **README files,** and how to use them effectively. We will also look at **real-world examples** of well-documented projects that follow best practices in documentation.

Writing Clear, Concise, and Helpful Documentation

Good documentation should be **clear, concise,** and **informative.** It serves as both an **instructional guide** and a **reference manual** for developers who will interact with the code. Well-documented code can be understood, used, and extended with minimal effort, even by developers who were not originally involved in the project.

1. Focus on the "Why" and "How"

Documentation should explain not only **what** the code does but also **why** it is doing it in a particular way. This is especially important for complex or non-intuitive logic, as it helps developers understand the reasoning behind certain design decisions.

- **What**: What does this function or class do?
- **Why**: Why was this particular approach or solution chosen?
- **How**: How is it implemented and how should it be used?

2. Be Concise but Complete

While documentation should be thorough, it should avoid unnecessary verbosity. Be **succinct** but make sure all essential details are included.

- Keep **function descriptions** to the point.
- For **complex algorithms**, provide a **high-level explanation** followed by relevant code snippets or pseudocode.

- Avoid unnecessary details that don't add value for the reader.

Bad Example:

cpp

```cpp
// This function adds two numbers and returns the
sum
int add(int a, int b) {
    return a + b;
}
```

This is overly simplistic, and the comment adds no real value.

Good Example:

cpp

```cpp
// Adds two integers and returns the sum.
// This function is designed to handle both
positive and negative integers efficiently.
// Parameters:
//   a: The first integer to add.
//   b: The second integer to add.
// Returns:
//   The sum of a and b.
int add(int a, int b) {
    return a + b;
}
```

This comment explains the function's behavior and parameters clearly without being overly verbose.

The Role of Documentation in Making Code Maintainable

Good documentation is a key factor in ensuring that code remains maintainable over time. It allows developers to easily **understand** and **extend** the code, reducing the chances of introducing errors when making changes or additions.

1. Enhances Understandability

For both **new developers** and **existing team members**, well-documented code provides a clear understanding of the logic behind the implementation. It serves as an instructional guide for anyone working on the codebase.

2. Facilitates Debugging and Refactoring

When issues arise or refactoring is needed, clear documentation helps developers quickly identify the purpose of each component of the code. It can also aid in ensuring that changes don't break functionality, as the documented **expected behavior** provides a reliable reference point.

3. Onboarding New Developers

When a new team member joins the project, documentation serves as a critical resource for getting up to speed with the codebase. A comprehensive set of documents can significantly reduce the learning curve for new developers, allowing them to be productive faster.

4. Preserves Knowledge

Documentation is particularly valuable in teams with high **turnover** or in open-source projects where contributors change frequently. By documenting the logic and thought process behind the code, developers ensure that important knowledge is preserved and easily accessible.

Using Docstrings, Comments, and README Files Effectively

While **docstrings**, **comments**, and **README files** all serve different purposes, they each play a role in ensuring that the code is easily understandable and maintainable.

1. Docstrings (For Functions, Classes, and Modules)

Docstrings are used to describe the purpose of a **function**, **class**, or **module**. In languages like **Python**, docstrings are placed directly below the function or class definition and provide an easy way to document how a piece of code should be used.

Best Practices for Writing Docstrings:

- Include a **short** **description** of what the function/class/module does.
- Document the **parameters** and their types.
- Include the **return value** and its type.
- If applicable, provide **examples** of usage.

Example:

python

```
def add(a, b):
    """
    Adds two numbers and returns the result.

    Parameters:
    a (int): The first number to add.
    b (int): The second number to add.

    Returns:
    int: The sum of a and b.
```

```
Example:
>>> add(3, 4)
7
"""
return a + b
```

2. Comments

Comments should be used to explain specific lines or blocks of code that may not be immediately obvious. However, comments should **not** replace writing clean, self-explanatory code. They should be used **sparingly** and **only when necessary**.

Best Practices for Comments:

- Use comments to **explain the "why"** behind decisions or complex logic.
- Avoid obvious comments like "Increment counter by 1" when the code is self-explanatory.
- Ensure comments are up-to-date with the code.

Example:

cpp

```cpp
// Using a greedy algorithm to minimize the cost
int minCost = calculateMinimumCost(); // Call to
calculate the minimum cost
```

Here, the comment clarifies the **approach** being used, which can be useful when the algorithm isn't straightforward.

3. README Files

A **README file** is often the first thing users or new developers see when interacting with a project. It serves as a guide to understanding the purpose of the project, how to get started, and how to contribute.

Best Practices for Writing README Files:

- **Project Overview**: A brief description of what the project is, its purpose, and its key features.
- **Installation Instructions**: Step-by-step instructions on how to set up the project locally.
- **Usage Examples**: Provide examples showing how to use the code or interact with the application.
- **Contribution Guidelines**: If the project is open-source, include guidelines for contributing.
- **Licenses and Acknowledgements**: Include any licenses or acknowledgements relevant to the project.

Example:

markdown

```
# My Web Application
```

Overview
This web application allows users to track their tasks and productivity. It is designed to help individuals stay organized and manage their time effectively.

Installation
1. Clone the repository: `git clone https://github.com/myrepo/my-web-app`
2. Install dependencies: `npm install`
3. Start the development server: `npm start`

Usage
Once the application is running, navigate to `http://localhost:3000` in your browser to view the homepage.

Contributing
1. Fork the repository
2. Create a feature branch (`git checkout -b feature/your-feature`)
3. Commit your changes
4. Push to your fork
5. Submit a pull request

License
MIT License

The README file offers a **clear guide** for installation, usage, and contribution, making it easy for developers to get started with the project.

Real-World Examples of Well-Documented Projects

1. React

The **React** JavaScript library is an excellent example of a well-documented open-source project. Its documentation includes:

- **Clear API documentation** with usage examples.
- **Conceptual explanations** to help developers understand the underlying principles of React.
- **Best practices** and **patterns** for writing maintainable React code.
- **Interactive tutorials** and a **developer community** to help users get up to speed.

2. Django

Django, a popular Python web framework, is another excellent example of a well-documented project. The Django documentation includes:

262

- **Detailed docstrings** for all modules, classes, and functions.
- **Clear examples** showing how to implement key features like models, views, and templates.
- **Installation instructions** and **best practices** for developing production-ready applications.

Conclusion

Effective **documentation** is an essential aspect of maintaining **clean code**. By writing **clear, concise, and helpful documentation**, developers can ensure that their code is understandable, maintainable, and easily extensible. **Docstrings, comments**, and **README files** all serve different purposes, but they should be used together to create an environment where code is not just written for immediate use but is also **accessible** and **easily understood** by others in the future. Real-world examples like **React** and **Django** show that excellent documentation is crucial for the success and longevity of a project, especially in collaborative or open-source environments.

CHAPTER 21

COLLABORATION AND COMMUNICATION FOR CLEAN CODE

The success of any software project depends not only on the individual skills of developers but also on how effectively teams **collaborate** and **communicate**. In the context of **clean code**, collaboration and communication are critical for maintaining consistency, enforcing coding standards, and ensuring that the codebase remains **maintainable** and **scalable** over time. In this chapter, we will explore how **team collaboration and communication** influence code quality, the tools and practices that facilitate **collaborative clean code development**, and the importance of **code standards and style guides** in team environments. Additionally, we will examine **real-world examples** of successful collaborative projects that prioritize clean code.

How Team Collaboration and Communication Influence Code Quality

Effective **collaboration** and **communication** among team members play a vital role in maintaining clean code throughout the software development lifecycle. When developers work together harmoniously, they can leverage each other's strengths and catch issues early in the development process, leading to higher-quality, more maintainable code.

1. Shared Knowledge and Consistency

When developers collaborate effectively, they share **knowledge** and ensure that everyone is on the same page regarding the **design principles**, **coding conventions**, and **best practices**. This consistency across the team helps maintain a uniform coding style, making it easier to read, understand, and extend the codebase. Without consistent communication, different developers might approach similar problems in vastly different ways, which can result in **spaghetti code** or redundant implementations.

Example:

In a team that practices good collaboration, if one developer writes a particularly efficient sorting function, others can learn from it and apply the same technique in their own code, leading to a more consistent approach across the project.

2. Early Bug Detection and Problem Solving

Through constant communication, developers can address issues early on, which prevents bugs from becoming larger problems down the road. Code reviews, pair programming, and daily stand-ups provide **opportunities to catch mistakes** early, share knowledge, and collaborate on solutions, improving overall code quality.

Example:

During a **pair programming session**, two developers might spot an inefficient algorithm and quickly come up with a more optimal solution. This early detection avoids **performance bottlenecks** and improves the code's efficiency before it becomes a problem.

3. Clearer Requirements and Expectations

Effective communication ensures that all team members understand the **project requirements**, the **technical challenges**, and the **desired outcomes**. This clarity helps developers write code that aligns with the project's goals and avoids miscommunication or redundant work. Regular meetings, discussions, and feedback loops foster a culture of transparency and mutual understanding.

Example:

A product owner clearly communicates the **new feature requirements** during a sprint planning session, allowing developers to build the functionality in a manner that **fits the larger system design**, preventing unnecessary refactoring later on.

Tools and Practices for Collaborative Clean Code Development

Modern software development relies on several tools and practices that facilitate collaborative clean code development. These tools help teams manage code quality, enforce standards, and communicate efficiently. Let's explore some of the most useful tools and practices for collaborative clean code development.

1. Version Control Systems (VCS)

A **Version Control System** (e.g., **Git**) is essential for collaboration, enabling multiple developers to work on different parts of the code simultaneously without causing conflicts. **Git** tracks changes to the codebase, allowing developers to view history, roll back changes, and merge code safely. It also makes collaboration more efficient by providing a **central repository** for all code.

Best Practices for Version Control:

- **Branching Strategies**: Use **feature branches** to develop new functionality and **pull requests** for code review before merging changes into the main branch.
- **Commit Often**: Encourage frequent commits with **small, meaningful changes**. This makes the code easier to review and reduces the likelihood of conflicts.
- **Write Meaningful Commit Messages**: Provide clear and concise commit messages that explain what was changed and why.

2. Continuous Integration/Continuous Deployment (CI/CD)

CI/CD pipelines automate the process of testing, building, and deploying code. By integrating **automated testing** into the CI/CD process, developers can catch bugs early and ensure that code quality is maintained across the project. These pipelines allow teams to deploy **incremental changes** to production continuously, making the development process more efficient and less error-prone.

Tools for CI/CD:

- **Jenkins**: A widely used open-source automation server for building and testing code.
- **GitLab CI**: Provides integrated CI/CD pipelines for projects hosted on GitLab.
- **CircleCI**: A cloud-based CI/CD platform that automates testing and deployment.

3. Code Review Tools

Code reviews are an essential practice for maintaining clean code and sharing knowledge. Tools like **GitHub Pull Requests**, **GitLab Merge Requests**, and **Bitbucket Pull Requests** make it easy to conduct code reviews, track feedback, and merge code changes. These tools allow team members to review and discuss code before it is merged into the main branch, ensuring that only clean, quality code makes it to production.

Best Practices for Code Reviews:

- **Provide Constructive Feedback**: Focus on **improving the code**, not criticizing the developer.
- **Review Small Changes**: Break down larger pull requests into smaller, more manageable chunks to make them easier to review.
- **Be Respectful**: Code reviews are about collaboration and learning, so approach them with respect and humility.

Working with Code Standards and Style Guides in Teams

Having clear **coding standards** and a **style guide** is essential for maintaining consistency across a project, especially in teams. A consistent coding style makes the codebase easier to read, understand, and maintain. It also reduces friction during code reviews and makes it easier for new developers to contribute.

1. Defining Code Standards

Creating and enforcing a set of **coding standards** ensures that the entire team adheres to best practices and conventions. Standards should cover areas such as:

- **Indentation**: Whether to use spaces or tabs, and how many spaces per indentation level.
- **Naming Conventions**: Whether to use **CamelCase**, **snake_case**, or other naming schemes for variables, functions, and classes.
- **File Organization**: Guidelines for organizing files and directories in a logical and predictable manner.

Example of Naming Conventions:

- Use **camelCase** for variables and functions (`userName`, `calculateTotal`).
- Use **PascalCase** for classes and interfaces (`UserManager`, `ProductService`).

2. Style Guides

A **style guide** is a set of rules that define how code should be written and formatted. This includes guidelines for code formatting, commenting, and structuring code in a readable and consistent manner. By following a style guide, the team ensures that the codebase remains easy to navigate, reducing the likelihood of introducing bugs due to misinterpretation of code.

Popular Style Guides:

- **Google Style Guides**: Provides comprehensive guidelines for languages like **C++**, **Python**, **Java**, and **JavaScript**.
- **Airbnb JavaScript Style Guide**: A popular style guide for JavaScript projects that emphasizes code readability and consistency.

271

Examples of Successful Collaborative Projects with Clean Code

1. Google's Open-Source Projects

Google's open-source projects are well-known for their **clean code** and **collaborative culture**. For example, **Google's Protocol Buffers** and **gRPC** are both **well-documented** and feature **consistent coding standards** that facilitate collaboration among global teams. Google uses strict **code review processes** to ensure that all code adheres to its internal **clean code practices**.

Success Factors:

- Use of **version control** and **CI/CD** pipelines to ensure code quality.
- **Clear documentation** and **coding standards** that all contributors follow.
- A strong culture of **feedback** and **mentorship** that helps new contributors adhere to best practices.

2. Mozilla Firefox

The Mozilla Firefox team has successfully maintained a large codebase while prioritizing **collaboration** and **clean code**. The project uses **Git** for version control, and all contributors must adhere to the project's **style guide** and **coding standards**.

272

Mozilla's open-source approach allows contributions from developers worldwide, ensuring the codebase remains maintainable and scalable.

Success Factors:

- **Automated testing** and **continuous integration** to catch bugs early.
- Regular **code reviews** and a focus on **high-quality documentation**.
- A strong community of developers and contributors that encourages collaboration and shared learning.

3. Django (Python Web Framework)

Django, a widely-used Python web framework, follows strict **coding standards** and ensures that its codebase remains clean and well-structured. Django's development process is highly **collaborative**, with **peer reviews** and **clear documentation** for all contributors.

Success Factors:

- **Clear and concise documentation** that covers everything from basic usage to advanced features.
- Consistent **coding style** and **naming conventions** across the project.

- A large **community** that actively participates in maintaining and improving the codebase.

Conclusion

Effective **collaboration** and **communication** are crucial for maintaining clean code in team environments. By using the right tools and practices—such as **version control, CI/CD pipelines, code review tools**, and **style guides**—teams can ensure that their code remains **consistent, maintainable**, and **scalable** over time. Real-world examples from successful projects like **Google's open-source initiatives, Mozilla Firefox**, and **Django** show that fostering a culture of collaboration and clean code can lead to high-quality software that is easier to manage and evolve. Clean code doesn't just happen on its own—it requires continuous communication, shared knowledge, and a commitment to best practices across the entire team.

CHAPTER 22

CONTINUOUS INTEGRATION AND CONTINUOUS DELIVERY (CI/CD)

In modern software development, **Continuous Integration** (CI) and **Continuous Delivery** (CD) are essential practices that ensure clean code and streamlined deployment processes. By automating various aspects of software development, testing, and deployment, CI/CD pipelines improve the efficiency of development workflows and significantly enhance **software quality**. This chapter explores the role of CI/CD in maintaining clean code, how automation helps streamline testing and deployment, and the benefits of integrating CI/CD pipelines into your development process. We will also look at **real-world examples** of successful CI/CD pipelines in practice.

The Role of CI/CD in Maintaining Clean Code

CI/CD plays a pivotal role in ensuring that code remains clean, functional, and deployable throughout the development lifecycle. The **continuous integration** process involves merging code changes into the main codebase frequently, while **continuous delivery** ensures that the code is automatically deployed to production or staging environments, often after successful tests.

1. Early Detection of Bugs and Issues

CI/CD pipelines help catch issues early by automatically running tests every time code is committed. This frequent testing enables developers to detect **bugs, performance issues**, or **integration problems** as soon as they occur, making it easier to fix them before they grow into more significant problems.

- **Frequent testing** allows developers to see the impact of their changes immediately, preventing bugs from being introduced into the main codebase.
- Automated tests reduce human error and help ensure that code remains stable as it evolves.

2. Improving Code Quality

CI/CD practices encourage writing **clean, testable code** because developers know their code will be automatically tested and deployed. This reduces the likelihood of **code rot** (when code becomes difficult to maintain over time) and ensures that every part of the codebase meets the required quality standards before it is merged.

- Clean code is a key outcome of frequent integration and delivery because it forces developers to adhere to best practices, such as writing small, modular, testable functions, and avoiding large, untested code dumps.

3. Consistency Across Development Environments

By integrating CI/CD into the development process, developers can ensure that the code behaves consistently across **development**, **staging**, and **production** **environments**. Automated deployment scripts ensure that the same configuration is used across all environments, reducing the chances of errors and discrepancies between environments.

Automating the Testing and Deployment of Clean Code

One of the most significant benefits of CI/CD is the ability to **automate** the testing and deployment processes, making it easier to maintain a clean codebase and ensure smooth transitions from development to production.

1. Automating Testing

Automated testing is a key component of CI/CD pipelines. It ensures that the code is **tested** at every stage of development, from **unit tests** to **integration tests** to **end-to-end tests**.

- **Unit Tests**: Run automatically with every change to ensure individual components are functioning correctly.
- **Integration Tests**: Validate that different parts of the application work together as expected.
- **End-to-End Tests**: Test the entire flow of the application, ensuring that the system works from the user's perspective.

By automating testing, teams can avoid the need for time-consuming manual testing and ensure that tests are always run on every change, regardless of the size of the codebase.

Example:

In a typical CI pipeline, when a developer pushes code to the repository, a series of tests are triggered:

1. **Unit tests** run to check the correctness of the individual components.
2. **Integration tests** check the interaction between components (e.g., database and API).

3. If the tests pass, the build moves to the **deployment** stage, where it is automatically pushed to a staging or production environment.

2. Automating Deployment

The goal of **continuous delivery** is to automate the deployment process so that software can be released at any time with minimal manual intervention. In this process, once the code passes all tests, it is automatically deployed to the appropriate environment—whether that's a **staging server** for further testing or a **production server** for live use.

By automating deployment:

- **Teams can release frequently**, reducing the risk of deployment errors and making the process more predictable.
- Developers and operations teams can spend less time manually configuring deployment environments and more time focusing on **writing clean code**.

Example:

Consider a web application being developed and deployed with CI/CD. The CI/CD pipeline:

1. Automatically pulls the latest code from the repository.

2. Runs **tests** to verify the integrity of the code.

3. If all tests pass, the application is automatically **deployed** to a test environment for further verification.

4. Once the tests in the staging environment are successful, the app is deployed to production, ensuring that **clean, tested code** is always available in the live environment.

How CI/CD Pipelines Improve Software Quality

CI/CD pipelines are integral to maintaining high software quality because they enforce consistent testing, quality checks, and smooth transitions between environments. Here's how CI/CD pipelines contribute to **better software quality**:

1. Consistent Code Testing

With CI/CD, **automated tests** are run on every code change, ensuring that the code is continually validated and tested. This provides **immediate feedback** to developers, enabling them to identify problems early and fix them before they affect other parts of the codebase.

*   Automated tests help catch **regressions** (previously fixed issues reappearing) and ensure that the latest code changes don't break existing functionality.

280

2. Faster Feedback Loop

CI/CD reduces the **feedback loop** between code changes and test results. Developers receive **immediate feedback** on the quality of their code, enabling them to take swift action if something breaks or behaves unexpectedly. This quick feedback ensures that the codebase remains **stable** and **reliable**.

- **Failing builds** notify the team that something has gone wrong, and the problem can be fixed before it becomes a bigger issue.

3. Reduced Human Error

Automating repetitive tasks like testing and deployment reduces the risk of **human error**. It ensures that each change is tested under the same conditions and that deployments are consistent across environments, which leads to fewer issues in production.

- Developers don't need to manually push code to the production server or check for deployment issues, as this is all handled by the CI/CD pipeline.

4. Improved Collaboration

CI/CD promotes better collaboration among teams by providing a clear structure for the software delivery process. **Development, testing**, and **operations teams** can collaborate seamlessly as they all work with the same automated pipeline. Everyone involved in the project knows when and where to find the most up-to-date version of the software, ensuring a smooth workflow.

Real-World Examples of CI/CD Pipelines in Practice

1. GitHub's CI/CD Pipeline

GitHub, one of the most popular platforms for hosting open-source projects, uses a robust CI/CD pipeline to maintain the quality of its software. Every time a pull request is submitted, GitHub automatically triggers:

- **Unit tests** for code correctness.
- **Integration tests** to check how changes interact with other parts of the system.
- **Code linting** to ensure code style consistency.
- **Deployment to staging** for further checks before pushing changes to production.

GitHub's use of **automated testing** and **CI/CD pipelines** ensures that only clean, verified code makes it to production, reducing the risk of bugs and downtime.

2. Netflix CI/CD Pipeline

Netflix, the global streaming giant, is renowned for its **microservices architecture** and **CI/CD pipeline**. They use CI/CD to deploy thousands of microservices across their infrastructure, ensuring that **new features** and **bug fixes** are deployed quickly and reliably.

Netflix employs a **continuous integration** strategy where code changes are continuously integrated into the main codebase, and their **continuous delivery pipeline** automatically deploys updates to production. Netflix also uses **Canary Releases** (gradually rolling out features to a small subset of users) to ensure that new changes don't disrupt the system.

Impact:

- Netflix's CI/CD pipeline allows them to **deploy new features quickly** while minimizing risk, ensuring that their users experience minimal disruption.
- Automated testing ensures that every service works correctly and integrates seamlessly with other services in the ecosystem.

3. CircleCI

CircleCI, a popular CI/CD service provider, has its own internal CI/CD pipeline that allows it to quickly build, test, and deploy new features and improvements. They use **GitHub repositories** for their code and **Docker containers** for building and testing software in isolated environments.

Impact:

- The CircleCI pipeline provides them with fast, **reliable testing** and **deployment**, allowing them to release updates regularly.
- **Automated deployment** to staging and production ensures that every change is thoroughly tested and integrated before it reaches users.

Conclusion

CI/CD is essential for maintaining **clean code** and ensuring **consistent quality** throughout the development lifecycle. By automating the processes of **testing**, **building**, and **deploying**, CI/CD pipelines allow teams to **deliver reliable**, **bug-free software** more efficiently. Through tools like **automated tests**, **version control systems**, and **deployment scripts**, CI/CD helps developers catch issues early, improve collaboration, and reduce human error. Real-world examples from companies like **GitHub**, **Netflix**, and **CircleCI** show how well-designed CI/CD pipelines enable faster software delivery without sacrificing quality. By implementing **CI/CD** in your own development process, you can achieve cleaner, more maintainable code that scales seamlessly with your application's needs.

CHAPTER 23

CLEAN CODE IN LEGACY SYSTEMS

Working with legacy systems is one of the most challenging aspects of software development. Legacy systems often come with **outdated architectures**, **unclean code**, and **complex dependencies** that make it difficult to implement changes or improvements. However, maintaining clean code within legacy systems is essential for their long-term sustainability and for the teams who will continue to work with the code. This chapter will explore the **challenges** of working with legacy code, strategies for introducing **clean code practices** into legacy systems, and the step-by-step process of **refactoring large codebases**. We will also look at **real-world case studies** of successful legacy system refactoring.

Challenges of Working with Legacy Code

Legacy systems are often **critical to business operations** and can represent a significant investment. However, they come with several challenges that make maintaining clean code difficult.

286

1. Lack of Documentation

Legacy systems often lack proper documentation, or the documentation may be outdated. This makes it harder to understand how the code works, what each part of the system does, and how the components interact with each other.

- **Impact**: Without proper documentation, it is easy to misinterpret the existing code, leading to bugs and inefficiencies. Additionally, new developers may struggle to understand the system quickly.

2. Outdated Technologies and Dependencies

Legacy systems often rely on old libraries, frameworks, and technologies that are no longer supported. Updating these dependencies can be risky and time-consuming, especially when the system is still in production.

- **Impact**: Upgrading old dependencies may break the code or introduce new bugs, making the transition difficult and costly.

3. Complex and Fragile Code

Legacy code tends to be more **monolithic**, with components tightly coupled and dependencies hard-coded. This increases the risk of making changes, as a modification in one part of the system may cause **unexpected failures** in other parts.

- **Impact**: It becomes difficult to introduce new features or changes without breaking existing functionality. As the system grows, the code becomes more **fragile** and harder to maintain.

4. Fear of Breaking Production

When dealing with legacy systems, there is often a fear of breaking production. Since these systems are essential to business operations, introducing changes without thoroughly testing them can lead to service interruptions or other critical issues.

- **Impact**: This leads to resistance to change and delays in updating or improving the system, which ultimately hampers the ability to introduce cleaner code practices.

Strategies for Introducing Clean Code Practices into Legacy Systems

Despite the challenges, it is possible to improve legacy code and bring it in line with clean code principles. The key is to **introduce changes incrementally** and prioritize **minimal risk** while improving maintainability. Here are some strategies to follow when introducing clean code into legacy systems:

1. Start with Automated Testing

One of the first steps in improving legacy code is to **write tests** for the existing system. Automated tests help ensure that new changes do not break the existing functionality.

- **Unit Tests**: Write tests for individual components to ensure that each unit of the code works as expected.
- **Integration Tests**: Focus on testing how different parts of the system interact with each other.
- **End-to-End Tests**: Simulate real-world user interactions to verify that the system works from start to finish.

By introducing automated tests, you create a safety net that allows you to make changes with confidence.

2. Incremental Refactoring

Rather than attempting a full rewrite of the legacy system, which can be risky and time-consuming, adopt an **incremental refactoring** approach. Refactor small parts of the system at a time, focusing on areas that are critical or have the most technical debt.

- **Refactor on the Fly**: Refactor code as you work on new features or bug fixes. Whenever you make a change, improve the code's design to make it cleaner and easier to understand.

- **Isolate Changes**: Break down large refactorings into smaller, isolated changes that minimize the risk of introducing bugs.

3. Apply the Boy Scout Rule

The **Boy Scout Rule** suggests that you should always leave the code in a better state than you found it. This means that every time you work with legacy code, aim to **improve its readability, simplicity, and structure**.

- **Simplify Complex Logic**: Identify areas with convoluted or duplicated logic and refactor them into smaller, more manageable pieces.
- **Rename Variables and Functions**: Use meaningful names that make the code easier to understand.
- **Eliminate Redundant Code**: Remove or refactor any duplicated code to improve maintainability.

4. Introduce Clean Code Practices Gradually

Implement clean code practices gradually, starting with the most critical areas. Focus on:

- Writing **self-explanatory code**.

- Following **naming conventions** and consistent **indentation**.
- Simplifying overly complex **functions** and **classes**.
- Removing or updating outdated libraries and dependencies.

Make clean code a **part of your development culture** so that future code is written according to best practices from the start.

Refactoring Large Codebases Step-by-Step

Refactoring a large legacy codebase requires a methodical approach. Here's a step-by-step process to help guide the refactoring efforts:

Step 1: Assess the Current State

Begin by assessing the **current state** of the codebase. Identify areas that need improvement, such as:

- Complex and fragile code.
- Duplicate code or unused components.
- Lack of tests or insufficient test coverage.

Step 2: Write Automated Tests

Before making any changes, write **automated tests** to cover the critical functionality of the codebase. This ensures that your refactorings don't break existing behavior.

- Start with **unit tests** for individual functions or methods.
- Expand to **integration tests** for testing interactions between components.
- Add **end-to-end tests** for overall system behavior.

Step 3: Begin Refactoring Small Sections

Start with **small, isolated sections** of the code that are easier to manage and refactor. Focus on one module or feature at a time and ensure that it works correctly before moving to the next.

- **Refactor functions** to make them smaller and more focused on a single responsibility.
- **Simplify logic** by removing unnecessary conditionals or loops.

Step 4: Continuously Test and Validate

As you refactor, run the automated tests regularly to ensure that the code still works as expected. If a test fails, investigate and fix the issue before proceeding further.

292

Step 5: Improve Code Structure and Design

After refactoring the basic functionality, focus on improving the **overall structure** of the code:

- Apply design patterns to improve flexibility and maintainability.
- Separate concerns using principles like **Separation of Concerns (SoC)** and **Single Responsibility Principle (SRP)**.
- Modularize the code to make it easier to test and extend.

Step 6: Monitor and Iterate

Refactoring is an ongoing process. After making improvements, continue to monitor the system and iterate on the changes. As new issues arise, refactor further to ensure the code remains clean and maintainable.

Case Studies of Successful Legacy System Refactoring

1. Spotify: Migrating to Microservices

Spotify faced the challenge of refactoring a **monolithic** codebase into a **microservices** architecture. The team used **incremental**

refactoring, breaking down the large codebase into smaller, more manageable pieces.

Process:

- Automated testing was added to ensure that refactoring didn't break existing features.
- A clear migration path was created for each service, allowing for gradual integration of new microservices while the old codebase was still operational.

Outcome:

- The migration to microservices improved **scalability** and allowed Spotify to deploy features faster.
- Clean code practices and automated testing ensured that the migration was smooth and didn't disrupt the user experience.

2. The Basecamp Redesign

Basecamp, a project management tool, underwent a significant redesign, which included refactoring a large codebase that had accumulated technical debt over time. The team applied **clean code principles** to make the system more maintainable and scalable.

Process:

- The team focused on improving **modularity** and **readability** by breaking large, complex methods and classes into smaller, more manageable pieces.
- The code was refactored in small steps to avoid overwhelming the development team and to ensure minimal disruption to the system.

Outcome:

- Basecamp's code became **cleaner** and easier to maintain, reducing the risk of bugs and enabling faster feature development.
- The refactoring process enhanced **team productivity** and fostered a better understanding of the system's structure.

Conclusion

Working with legacy systems is challenging, but with the right strategies and a step-by-step approach to **refactoring**, you can introduce clean code practices that improve the system's maintainability and scalability. By starting with **automated tests**, refactoring **incrementally**, and applying clean code principles gradually, legacy systems can be transformed into well-structured, easy-to-manage codebases. The examples from **Spotify** and

Basecamp show that even large, complex legacy systems can be refactored successfully, providing long-term benefits for both developers and users.

CHAPTER 24

WRITING CLEAN CODE FOR LARGE-SCALE SYSTEMS

Writing clean code is a challenge in any software project, but it becomes exponentially more difficult when working with **large-scale systems**. As systems grow in size, complexity increases, and maintaining clean, understandable, and maintainable code can feel overwhelming. However, applying **clean code practices** can significantly improve the structure, **scalability**, and **maintainability** of large applications. This chapter will explore how to **handle complexity** in large codebases, organize code for **scalability** and **maintainability**, and modularize large applications to improve **code management**. We will also look at real-world examples of successful clean code practices in large-scale **enterprise applications**.

Handling Complexity in Large Codebases

As software systems grow, they become more complex, often leading to what is known as **code bloat** or **spaghetti code**—a situation where the codebase becomes entangled, difficult to read, and even harder to modify. Handling complexity is one of the most critical aspects of maintaining clean code in large systems.

1. Decompose Large Systems into Manageable Components

To handle complexity, it's essential to **decompose** a large codebase into smaller, more manageable components. This is where practices like **modular programming**, **separation of concerns**, and **design patterns** come into play.

- **Modularization**: Break down the system into modules or services that each handle a specific responsibility. This ensures that each module can be developed, tested, and maintained independently.

- **Separation of Concerns (SoC)**: Keep different aspects of the system (e.g., data access, business logic, UI) separate from each other. This reduces interdependencies and makes it easier to manage complexity.

2. Apply Design Patterns

Design patterns like **MVC** (Model-View-Controller), **Factory**, **Singleton**, and **Observer** can help manage complexity by providing standard solutions to common problems. These patterns ensure that the code is structured in a way that is **extensible**, **flexible**, and **easy to maintain**.

Example:

In a large-scale **e-commerce platform**, the **Factory Pattern** can be used to create different types of payment methods (credit card, PayPal, etc.). This allows the system to be easily extended to support additional payment methods without disrupting the existing codebase.

3. Avoid Premature Optimization

Large systems can become difficult to manage if you attempt to optimize everything from the start. **Premature optimization** can lead to complex code with little benefit. Focus on **clean code** first and optimize for performance only when there is a proven need.

- **Refactor** first to improve readability and structure.
- Use **profiling tools** (e.g., **gprof, Valgrind**) to identify performance bottlenecks before applying optimizations.

4. Emphasize Readability

In large systems, **readability** is essential. Code should be written in such a way that anyone on the team can understand it quickly. This means using **clear variable names, consistent formatting**, and **well-organized functions**.

Organizing Code for Scalability and Maintainability

Organizing your code properly is key to scaling and maintaining large systems. **Code organization** ensures that the system is **easy to navigate**, **extend**, and **debug** as it grows.

1. Use Layered Architecture

In large systems, using a **layered architecture** (e.g., **presentation layer**, **business logic layer**, **data access layer**) helps separate concerns and ensures that each layer is responsible for specific functionality. This approach improves scalability by allowing different layers to evolve independently.

- **Presentation Layer**: Handles user interface and user interaction.
- **Business Logic Layer**: Contains the core functionality and business rules.
- **Data Access Layer**: Manages interactions with databases and external systems.

2. Use Dependency Injection (DI)

Dependency Injection helps manage dependencies in large systems by decoupling components. With DI, components don't directly instantiate their dependencies; instead, dependencies are injected by an external framework.

- **Benefit**: DI makes it easier to **replace** or **mock** dependencies for testing purposes, improving maintainability.
- **Example**: In a large-scale system, a **PaymentService** might rely on external payment gateways. Instead of hardcoding the payment gateway implementation into the service, use DI to inject different gateway implementations, allowing for easier switching or testing.

3. Maintain Consistent Coding Standards

Consistency is crucial when writing clean code in large systems. Using a **style guide** for naming conventions, formatting, and architecture patterns helps maintain consistency across the entire codebase.

- **Naming Conventions**: Use **descriptive names** for classes, methods, and variables.
- **Code Formatting**: Follow consistent rules for indentation, line breaks, and spacing.
- **Code Comments**: Use comments sparingly and only when necessary to explain complex logic.

Modularizing a Large Application for Better Code Management

Modularization is key to managing complexity in large applications. By breaking down the code into smaller, independent modules, teams can work more effectively, improve testability, and scale the system more easily.

1. Divide the Code into Small, Independent Modules

When building large applications, divide the system into **small, independent modules** or **microservices** (if adopting a microservices architecture). Each module should be focused on a single responsibility and should have clear input and output interfaces.

- **Example**: In a large enterprise system, the **Order Management System (OMS)** could be a separate module from the **Inventory System**. These modules should have well-defined APIs for interaction.

2. Use APIs for Communication

When modules or services interact, it's crucial to define clear, **well-documented APIs**. APIs act as the contract between different parts of the system and make it easier to replace, extend, or scale individual components without affecting the rest of the system.

- **Example**: In a **large-scale e-commerce platform**, the **Product Catalog** module might expose an API for retrieving product details. The **Order Service** can then interact with the catalog through this API, without worrying about the underlying implementation.

3. Keep Dependencies Between Modules Minimal

To make modularization effective, ensure that the dependencies between modules are **minimal** and **well-defined**. **Loose coupling** between modules helps reduce complexity and makes it easier to maintain and scale the system.

- **Benefit**: Minimizing dependencies allows individual modules to evolve independently and simplifies the process of updating or replacing parts of the system.

Real-World Examples of Clean Code in Large-Scale Enterprise Applications

1. Amazon Web Services (AWS)

Amazon's **AWS** platform is one of the most well-known examples of clean code practices in a large-scale system. AWS handles a massive amount of traffic, and its architecture is designed to scale effectively while maintaining clean code.

- **Microservices Architecture**: AWS uses a **microservices-based** architecture, where individual services are modular, independently scalable, and loosely coupled.
- **API-First Design**: Each microservice exposes a well-defined API for communication, ensuring that different services can interact with each other seamlessly.

Impact:

- AWS can scale its services independently, allowing for **efficient resource management** and the ability to roll out new features without disrupting existing services.
- **Clean, modular code** ensures that AWS can handle high traffic while maintaining high availability.

2. Uber

Uber, a **ride-sharing service**, operates a highly complex system that handles millions of trips per day. Uber's codebase is built around a **service-oriented architecture (SOA)**, with individual services responsible for specific business functions like ride matching, payment processing, and location tracking.

- **Microservices**: Uber has migrated towards a **microservices architecture**, enabling its system to scale horizontally by adding more services as demand grows.
- **Service Discovery**: Uber uses tools like **Consul** for service discovery, allowing services to dynamically locate each other, which improves scalability and flexibility.

Impact:

- Uber can scale its services independently, allowing them to handle sudden spikes in demand during peak hours.
- **Modularization** and **independent service development** enable Uber's development teams to release features faster and more safely.

3. Google Search

Google Search is one of the most scalable and reliable systems in the world, capable of handling billions of queries every day. The system is built using principles of **clean code** and **modularization**.

- **Distributed Systems**: Google Search uses a highly **distributed system** with independent modules handling different aspects like crawling, indexing, and ranking.
- **Fault Tolerance**: The system is designed to handle failures gracefully, with each module being **independently recoverable** in case of failure.

Impact:

- Google Search can process an **immense volume of data** while remaining fast and highly available.
- The **modular design** allows individual components to evolve and scale independently, ensuring continuous improvement without disrupting service.

Conclusion

Writing clean code for large-scale systems requires careful planning, modularization, and an emphasis on scalability and maintainability. By applying principles like **modular programming**, **separation of concerns**, and **service-oriented architectures**, developers can manage the inherent complexity of large codebases while maintaining a high standard of clean code. Real-world examples from companies like **Amazon**, **Uber**, and **Google** show that well-structured, modular systems can scale effectively, adapt to growing user demands, and remain maintainable over time. By following these principles, you can write clean code for large-scale systems that are efficient, flexible, and easy to maintain.

CHAPTER 25

ADOPTING CLEAN CODE PRACTICES IN YOUR TEAM

Adopting **clean code practices** within a development team is not just about writing better code; it's about fostering a **culture** of **quality, collaboration**, and **continuous improvement**. As a team, adopting clean code principles can enhance productivity, reduce defects, and make the codebase more maintainable in the long term. This chapter will explore how to **introduce clean code principles** to your development team, establish **coding standards** and **best practices**, and create a team culture focused on **continuous improvement**. We will also examine **real-world examples** of teams that successfully adopted clean code practices and the positive impact it had on their software quality.

Introducing Clean Code Principles to Your Development Team

The first step in adopting clean code practices is **introducing the principles** to your development team. This process requires more than simply mandating rules—it involves **educating** the team on the importance of clean code and its long-term benefits.

1. Start with Education and Awareness

Before implementing any changes, take the time to **educate** your team about the **importance of clean code** and its principles. A good starting point is to **read books** like **"Clean Code" by Robert C. Martin** or watch videos and tutorials that focus on clean code practices.

- **Organize Training Sessions**: Hold regular **workshops** or **lunch-and-learn sessions** to explain the key concepts of clean code. Make sure these sessions cover topics like **naming conventions, code readability, modularity**, and **SOLID principles**.
- **Show Real-World Examples**: Present examples of both **clean** and **unclean code** to highlight the differences and show how the quality of code impacts maintenance, debugging, and scalability.

2. Set Clear Goals and Expectations

It's essential to **define clear goals** for the team and communicate **why** adopting clean code practices matters. Explain how clean code leads to improved collaboration, faster bug fixing, and a more efficient development process.

- **Set measurable goals**: For example, aim to reduce **code complexity** by a certain percentage or increase the **test coverage** in the codebase.
- **Provide feedback**: Set up processes like **code reviews** or **pair programming** to ensure adherence to clean code principles and provide constructive feedback.

3. Lead by Example

Leadership plays a crucial role in adopting clean code practices. As a team lead or manager, you must **lead by example**. Demonstrate clean code principles in your own work and in the decisions you make.

- **Write clean code** yourself and encourage others to ask questions when something seems unclear.
- **Encourage team members** to review each other's code for quality and to suggest improvements.

Establishing Coding Standards and Best Practices

To maintain clean code consistently across the team, it is essential to **establish coding standards** and best practices. Clear guidelines ensure that everyone is on the same page, leading to more readable, maintainable, and consistent code.

310

1. Define Clear and Consistent Coding Standards

Your team needs a **set of coding standards** that define how code should be written and structured. These standards should be comprehensive, covering everything from naming conventions to function length.

- **Naming Conventions**: Set rules for naming variables, functions, and classes, ensuring consistency across the codebase. For example, use **camelCase** for variables and functions and **PascalCase** for classes.
- **Indentation and Spacing**: Ensure that everyone follows a **consistent indentation style** (e.g., 2 or 4 spaces) and proper spacing between logical code blocks to enhance readability.
- **Commenting and Documentation**: Define when and how to use comments and docstrings. Comments should explain **why** the code does something, not **what** it's doing (as the latter should be clear from the code itself).

2. Use Style Guides and Linters

A style guide provides a comprehensive set of coding conventions and **best practices** for the team to follow. Tools like **linters** and **formatters** can help enforce these conventions by automatically checking for style violations.

- **Tools like ESLint (JavaScript), Checkstyle (Java)**, and **Pylint (Python)** can be integrated into the build process to flag violations of coding standards.
- **Prettier** can be used to automatically format code according to the team's style guidelines, ensuring consistency without the need for manual formatting.

3. Define Best Practices

In addition to coding standards, it's essential to establish **best practices** for writing clean, maintainable code. Best practices should include principles such as:

- **Write small, focused functions**: Functions should perform only one task and do it well.
- **Avoid duplication**: Refactor redundant code and use functions or classes to reuse common logic.
- **Write meaningful unit tests**: Ensure that code is covered by automated tests that verify functionality and catch regressions.

Creating a Team Culture of Continuous Improvement

Adopting clean code principles is not a one-time task—it requires **ongoing effort** and a **continuous improvement mindset**. Creating a culture of clean code within your team is about encouraging **constant learning**, **feedback**, and **collaboration**.

1. Promote Pair Programming and Code Reviews

Pair programming and **code reviews** are two excellent practices that help improve code quality, share knowledge, and ensure adherence to clean code principles.

- **Pair Programming**: In pair programming, two developers work together on the same piece of code, often with one writing and the other reviewing. This promotes **collaboration** and encourages learning between team members.
- **Code Reviews**: Encourage regular **code reviews** where team members can review each other's code for readability, correctness, and adherence to clean code practices. Make sure that reviews are constructive and focused on **improving** the code, not criticizing the developer.

2. Foster a Growth Mindset

Encourage team members to adopt a **growth mindset**, where they view coding challenges and mistakes as opportunities to learn and improve. Celebrate **small wins** and incremental improvements in code quality to keep the team motivated.

- **Retrospectives**: Hold regular team retrospectives to discuss what's working well in terms of code quality and where improvements can be made.
- **Encourage knowledge sharing**: Organize internal **knowledge-sharing sessions**, where team members can discuss clean code principles, share experiences, and learn from each other's successes and failures.

3. Focus on Incremental Improvement

Adopting clean code practices should be a gradual process. Instead of trying to refactor everything at once, encourage incremental improvements. Each developer should aim to leave the code in a better state than they found it.

- **The Boy Scout Rule**: "Always leave the campground cleaner than you found it" applies to code as well. Developers should aim to improve code readability, reduce complexity, and eliminate technical debt wherever possible.

Examples of Teams That Successfully Adopted Clean Code Practices

1. GitHub

GitHub's engineering team emphasizes the importance of **clean, readable code** and **collaboration**. The team regularly conducts **code reviews**, uses **consistent code formatting**, and maintains high standards for code documentation. GitHub's culture of **continuous improvement** has helped them scale their platform while ensuring the codebase remains clean and maintainable.

How GitHub Does It:

- **Code Reviews**: Every pull request undergoes a rigorous code review process where colleagues provide feedback on readability, test coverage, and adherence to coding standards.
- **Documentation**: GitHub's developers are encouraged to write **clear documentation** for every feature, making it easy for others to understand and extend the code.

2. Shopify

Shopify's development team adopted clean code practices early on in their journey to scale their e-commerce platform. They focus heavily on writing **modular** code that can easily scale as they continue to add features. Shopify also fosters a culture of **continuous improvement** through pair programming and regular refactoring sprints.

315

How Shopify Does It:

- **Modularization**: Shopify's architecture is designed around **microservices**, which allows individual components of their system to evolve independently while maintaining code cleanliness.
- **Collaboration**: Developers work together using **pair programming** to review and improve code before it's merged into the main codebase.

3. Basecamp

Basecamp's development team follows **clean code principles** and emphasizes **simplicity** in both their architecture and code. They prioritize **small, focused modules** and make use of **unit testing** to ensure each piece of functionality is correctly implemented.

How Basecamp Does It:

- **Simplicity**: Basecamp's developers focus on **keeping things simple** and avoid over-engineering features. They prefer **minimalist solutions** that are easy to maintain and scale.
- **Test-Driven Development (TDD)**: They use TDD to ensure that code is both reliable and testable, preventing regressions and ensuring long-term maintainability.

Conclusion

Adopting clean code practices within a development team is essential for producing high-quality, maintainable software. By **introducing clean code principles**, establishing **coding standards**, and fostering a **culture of continuous improvement**, teams can ensure that their codebase remains **scalable**, **understandable**, and **easy to maintain**. Successful teams like **GitHub**, **Shopify**, and **Basecamp** demonstrate the positive impact of clean code practices on software development. With ongoing education, collaboration, and a commitment to writing clean code, any team can achieve higher standards of software quality, leading to better outcomes for both developers and end users.

CHAPTER 26

TOOLS AND LIBRARIES FOR WRITING CLEAN CODE

In modern software development, **tools and libraries** are invaluable in helping developers maintain clean, readable, and maintainable code. These tools assist with various aspects of development, from enforcing **coding standards** to ensuring **performance optimization**. In this chapter, we'll explore the **Integrated Development Environments (IDEs)**, **linters**, **formatters**, **static analysis tools**, **profiling tools**, and **popular libraries** that help you write cleaner, more efficient code. These tools not only streamline the development process but also help maintain consistent, high-quality software.

IDEs and Tools That Help You Write Clean, Maintainable Code

Integrated Development Environments (**IDEs**) and specialized tools can significantly improve the way you write and manage code. They provide **syntax highlighting**, **auto-completion**, **error checking**, and other features that contribute to cleaner code.

318

1. IDEs: The Backbone of Clean Code Development

IDEs are essential for writing clean code. A good IDE will integrate multiple tools that automate many tasks, such as code formatting, error detection, and debugging. Popular IDEs include:

- **Visual Studio Code**: A lightweight, highly customizable IDE that supports a variety of programming languages and integrates well with tools like **ESLint, Prettier**, and **Git**. It also offers intelligent code suggestions and quick fixes.

- **JetBrains IntelliJ IDEA**: A feature-rich IDE that supports many programming languages, offering smart code completion, refactoring tools, and seamless integration with version control and testing frameworks. It is particularly popular for **Java**, **Kotlin**, and **C++** development.

- **Eclipse**: Another popular IDE, especially for **Java** and **C++**. It offers integrated tools for debugging, refactoring, and working with version control systems. Eclipse also has numerous plugins for adding more functionality.

- **PyCharm**: For Python developers, PyCharm provides intelligent code completion, project navigation, and built-in testing support, all of which help developers write clean, efficient Python code.

Features of IDEs That Promote Clean Code:

- **Code refactoring**: IDEs like **IntelliJ IDEA** and **Visual Studio Code** offer refactoring tools that allow you to restructure code without changing its functionality.
- **Real-time error detection**: IDEs can highlight issues with the code as you type, catching syntax and semantic errors early in the development process.
- **Version control integration**: Most IDEs integrate with **Git**, allowing you to manage code versions and collaborate more effectively.

Linters, Formatters, and Static Analysis Tools

To ensure that your code follows **coding standards** and **best practices**, you can use linters, formatters, and static analysis tools. These tools automatically check your code for errors, style violations, and potential performance issues.

1. Linters

A **linter** is a tool that analyzes code for potential errors, code style issues, and possible bugs. Linters help enforce consistency across your codebase and ensure that all team members follow the same **coding conventions**.

- **ESLint**: A popular linter for JavaScript and TypeScript that checks for stylistic issues, common errors, and anti-patterns in your code.
- **Pylint**: A linter for Python that checks for errors, enforces coding standards, and detects potential bugs or performance issues.
- **Rubocop**: A static code analyzer and linter for Ruby that ensures compliance with Ruby style guides and detects errors in your code.

Benefits of Linters:

- Catch **syntax errors** and **logical mistakes** early.
- **Enforce coding standards** (naming conventions, indentation, etc.) automatically.
- Help new team members adhere to **team coding guidelines** without needing manual intervention.

2. Code Formatters

Code formatters automatically adjust your code's **style** and **formatting** to meet specific guidelines. They ensure consistent spacing, indentation, and alignment, which helps improve code readability.

- **Prettier**: A popular formatter for JavaScript, HTML, CSS, and other web technologies. Prettier formats your code to adhere to a consistent style, reducing formatting issues during code reviews.

- **Black**: A formatter for Python that automatically formats your code according to **PEP 8** guidelines. This eliminates the need for manual code formatting and ensures consistency.

Benefits of Code Formatters:

- Ensure **consistent style** across the codebase, making it easier for developers to read and understand the code.
- Save time by automatically formatting code according to pre-defined rules, freeing up time for more important development tasks.

3. Static Analysis Tools

Static analysis tools analyze your code without executing it. These tools look for potential **bugs**, **security vulnerabilities**, **performance bottlenecks**, and **other issues** in the code.

- **SonarQube**: An open-source static analysis tool that supports multiple programming languages and checks for code quality, bugs, security vulnerabilities, and code smells.
- **CodeClimate**: An automated code review tool that integrates with **GitHub** and provides feedback on maintainability, code coverage, and potential issues.

Benefits of Static Analysis Tools:

- Identify and fix **complexity** and **code smells** that make code hard to maintain.
- Detect potential **security vulnerabilities** before they become critical issues.
- Improve code **maintainability** and **quality** over time by enforcing quality checks.

Code Profiling and Optimization Tools

Once the code is written and functional, the next step is to ensure that it **performs well**. **Profiling tools** help developers identify **performance bottlenecks** in their code, such as **slow database queries**, **inefficient algorithms**, or **high memory consumption**.

1. Profiling Tools

Profiling tools help you monitor and measure the performance of your code by identifying which parts of the system are consuming the most resources.

- **gProfiler**: A powerful profiling tool for **C++**, **Java**, and other languages that allows you to visualize CPU usage and pinpoint performance bottlenecks.

- **Xdebug**: A PHP profiler and debugger that provides detailed information on the execution of PHP code, including time and memory usage.
- **VisualVM**: A monitoring, troubleshooting, and profiling tool for Java applications. VisualVM allows you to track CPU usage, memory consumption, and thread activity.

Benefits of Profiling Tools:

- **Identify bottlenecks** in performance and memory usage.
- Provide **insights into execution time** for specific parts of the code.
- Optimize system **resources** and make the code run faster and more efficiently.

2. Optimization Tools

Optimization tools help ensure that the application performs well under **high load** and remains responsive. These tools can help you analyze performance and make improvements where needed.

- **JProfiler**: A Java profiling tool that helps developers optimize the performance of Java applications by detecting memory leaks, thread issues, and CPU bottlenecks.
- **Valgrind**: A tool for **C/C++** programs that helps detect memory leaks, memory management problems, and performance issues.

Benefits of Optimization Tools:

- Help identify and eliminate **resource hogs**, improving the performance of your application.
- Provide detailed insights into **memory usage** and **runtime performance**, allowing for targeted optimization.
- **Reduce latency** and improve **scalability** by optimizing inefficient code paths.

Popular Libraries and Frameworks for Writing Clean, Reusable Code

Writing **clean** and **reusable code** is crucial for maintaining long-term code quality, especially in large systems. Leveraging the right libraries and frameworks can help you build modular, efficient, and well-structured code.

1. Libraries for Clean, Reusable Code

Libraries provide pre-written code that addresses common tasks and problems, allowing developers to focus on the unique aspects of their applications. When used properly, libraries promote **reusability** and **consistency** in your code.

- **Lodash (JavaScript)**: A modern utility library that provides a set of tools for working with arrays, objects, and functions. Lodash simplifies tasks like deep cloning, merging objects, and performing common data manipulations.

- **Guava (Java)**: A set of libraries for **Java** that provide a wide range of utilities for collections, caching, concurrency, and functional programming.

- **NumPy (Python)**: A powerful library for **numerical computations** in Python. NumPy makes working with large, multi-dimensional arrays and matrices easy and efficient, promoting cleaner, more readable code for data-heavy applications.

2. Frameworks for Building Maintainable Systems

Frameworks provide a structured approach to building applications and promote clean, maintainable code by enforcing best practices and design patterns.

- **Spring Framework (Java)**: A comprehensive framework for building **enterprise-level** Java applications. It encourages the use of **dependency injection**, **modular design**, and **separation of concerns**, leading to more maintainable systems.

- **Django (Python)**: A high-level Python framework that promotes rapid development and clean code by encouraging the use of **reusable components** and **built-in best practices** like authentication and form handling.

- **Angular (JavaScript/TypeScript)**: A front-end framework for building **single-page applications (SPAs)** that enforces modularity, **component-based architecture**, and clean separation between logic, view, and state.

Conclusion

Tools and libraries are essential for maintaining clean, efficient, and maintainable code. **IDEs** like **Visual Studio Code** and **IntelliJ IDEA** offer powerful features to help you write and manage clean code. **Linters** like **ESLint** and **Pylint, static analysis tools** like **SonarQube**, and **profiling tools** like **gProfiler** and **Valgrind** help enforce coding standards, detect errors, and optimize performance. Finally, **libraries** and **frameworks** like **Lodash, Spring**, and **Django** help you write clean, reusable code that can scale as your system grows. By incorporating these tools into your development process, you can ensure that your code remains high-quality, maintainable, and optimized throughout the software lifecycle.

CHAPTER 27

THE FUTURE OF CLEAN CODE: TRENDS AND EVOLVING PRACTICES

The landscape of software development is rapidly evolving, with new technologies, methodologies, and practices constantly reshaping the way we write code. As the industry adapts to these changes, **clean code practices** are also evolving to meet the demands of modern development. In this chapter, we will explore how **clean code practices** are adapting to new technology trends, the rise of **functional programming**, the influence of **AI and machine learning** on software quality, and how clean code will continue to shape development methodologies in the future.

How Clean Code Practices Are Evolving with New Technology Trends

As technology progresses, the nature of software development also changes. New trends and tools are constantly emerging, and these shifts often necessitate updates to traditional clean code practices. While the core principles of clean code remain relevant, how we apply them can evolve with the times.

1. Increased Focus on Automation

In the past, maintaining clean code required significant manual effort, such as reviewing code, refactoring, and ensuring compliance with standards. However, with the rise of automation tools, developers now have more support in enforcing clean code practices.

- **Automated testing** tools like **unit tests, integration tests,** and **continuous integration pipelines** (CI) help ensure that code changes do not break functionality and that the code remains **stable** and **scalable**.
- **Static analysis tools** such as **SonarQube** and **CodeClimate** now provide more comprehensive feedback, catching style violations, performance bottlenecks, and potential bugs with minimal human effort.
- **Auto-formatting** tools like **Prettier** and **Black** allow developers to focus on the logic of their code, knowing that formatting will be handled automatically.

As automation continues to improve, **manual interventions** in code maintenance and quality control will decrease, making clean code practices more efficient and less error-prone.

329

2. Microservices Architecture

The adoption of **microservices architecture** has become a popular trend in modern software development. Microservices allow applications to be broken down into **smaller, independent services** that can be developed, deployed, and scaled individually.

- **Clean code practices** in microservices focus on **modularity** and **separation of concerns**. Each microservice should be responsible for a specific functionality, and **API contracts** help define the interactions between them.
- As teams work on independent services, **code consistency** and **standards** are crucial for maintaining readability and collaboration across services.

The increasing shift towards microservices means that clean code will need to focus even more on **modular design**, **clear interfaces**, and **scalability**.

The Rise of Functional Programming and Its Impact on Clean Code

Functional programming (FP) has seen a resurgence in popularity, especially in languages like **JavaScript**, **Python**, **Scala**, and

Haskell. FP offers a different approach to writing code compared to **imperative programming**, and its emphasis on **immutability**, **pure functions**, and **first-class functions** can have a significant impact on clean code practices.

1. Emphasis on Pure Functions

In functional programming, the use of **pure functions**—functions that have no side effects and always return the same output for the same input—encourages cleaner code. These functions are easier to test and reason about, as they do not rely on external states or mutate data.

- **Clean code in FP** means writing small, **pure functions** that each perform one well-defined task, improving code **readability** and **maintainability**.

2. Immutability and Avoiding Side Effects

FP emphasizes **immutability**, where data cannot be modified after it's created. This helps avoid common bugs related to changing shared state and makes code more predictable.

- Clean code in the FP world means using **immutable data structures** and ensuring that functions do not have side effects, making the system easier to reason about and test.

331

3. Higher-Order Functions and Composition

FP encourages the use of **higher-order functions** (functions that take other functions as arguments or return functions). This promotes **function composition**, where small, reusable functions are combined to build more complex functionality.

- In the clean code context, **composition over inheritance** is a practice that enables developers to build flexible systems without bloating the codebase with unnecessary dependencies or hierarchies.

As functional programming becomes more widely adopted, clean code practices will continue to evolve by incorporating these principles of **immutability**, **purity**, and **composition** to create more concise and maintainable software.

AI, Machine Learning, and Their Influence on Software Quality

Artificial Intelligence (AI) and Machine Learning (ML) are transforming almost every industry, and software development is no exception. As AI and ML are integrated into software systems, they can impact how developers write and maintain clean code, both directly and indirectly.

1. AI-Assisted Code Generation

AI-powered tools like **GitHub Copilot** use machine learning to **suggest code snippets** and complete functions based on context. These tools can help developers write cleaner code faster by recommending **best practices**, **standard libraries**, and more efficient algorithms.

- **Clean code practices** may be further automated with AI assistance, helping developers write more efficient, readable code without having to manually search for solutions or write boilerplate code.

2. AI for Code Reviews and Refactoring

AI-driven code review tools are becoming more capable of analyzing code quality and suggesting improvements. These tools can automatically identify **code smells**, **anti-patterns**, and **complex functions**, helping developers refactor their code without human intervention.

- AI-based tools will not only help developers write cleaner code but also provide **continuous feedback** during the development process, reinforcing best practices and making code quality management more automated.

3. Machine Learning for Performance Optimization

ML algorithms can be used to analyze software performance and suggest optimizations. For example, ML models can identify **bottlenecks** in code, recommend ways to improve **memory usage**, and optimize algorithms dynamically based on real-time usage data.

- **Clean code principles** will be complemented by AI-driven optimization, enabling developers to write code that is both clean and efficient at scale.

4. AI for Automated Testing

Machine learning can also assist in **automating tests**, particularly **regression tests** and **unit tests**, by learning from existing codebases and predicting the test coverage needed. AI can help detect edge cases and create tests that ensure the system behaves as expected under a variety of conditions.

- This will reduce the burden on developers to write exhaustive test cases and allow teams to focus on writing cleaner, more modular code that is easy to test.

The Future of Clean Code in the Context of Modern Development Methodologies

334

As development methodologies continue to evolve, clean code will adapt to meet the needs of modern teams, projects, and technologies. The integration of **Agile**, **DevOps**, **CI/CD**, and **microservices** into the software development lifecycle will require continuous attention to clean code principles.

1. Agile Development and Clean Code

In **Agile** development, the focus is on delivering working software frequently, with an emphasis on **short iterations** and **continuous feedback**. To maintain clean code in an Agile environment, developers must adopt practices like **TDD** (Test-Driven Development) and **refactoring** within each sprint.

- **Refactoring** and **pair programming** are key Agile practices that help keep the codebase clean and maintainable, ensuring that each increment of functionality is **well-tested** and **extensible**.

2. DevOps and Continuous Delivery

With **DevOps** and **CI/CD** practices, code is continuously integrated, tested, and deployed. To ensure that clean code practices are maintained in such fast-paced environments, automated testing, **static analysis**, and **refactoring** become even more critical.

- Developers will need to rely heavily on **automation tools** for testing and code quality enforcement to maintain clean code while rapidly deploying features.

3. Microservices and Clean Code

In a **microservices architecture**, each service is a self-contained unit with its own functionality. Clean code principles in this context will focus on **modular design, clear API contracts**, and **separation of concerns** between services.

- Developers will need to embrace **service-oriented design** and ensure that each microservice is **well-defined**, **maintainable**, and **testable**. The modular nature of microservices promotes clean code practices by enforcing smaller, focused codebases.

Conclusion

The future of clean code is intertwined with the evolving landscape of software development. As new technologies such as **AI, machine learning**, and **functional programming** reshape the way we write and maintain code, clean code practices will continue to evolve to incorporate these innovations. Tools for **automated testing, profiling**, and **AI-assisted code generation** will make writing clean, efficient code faster and more accessible.

As software systems become more complex, adopting clean code principles within **Agile**, **DevOps**, and **microservices** methodologies will ensure that code remains **maintainable**, **scalable**, and **efficient**. The future of clean code is bright, and by embracing these trends, developers can ensure that their software continues to meet the high standards required for modern, high-quality applications.